God: The Ultimate Lover

Learn how much God truly loves you!

Aaron Beach

Copyright and Fair-use

King James Version (KJV) and Young's Literal Translation (YLT) are in the public domain.

The Christian Standard Bible. Copyright © 2017 by Holman Bible Publishers. Used by permission. Christian Standard Bible®, and CSB® are federally registered trademarks of Holman Bible Publishers, all rights reserved.

Scriptures marked (ERV) are taken from the Easy-to-Read Version. Used by permission. Copyright © 2006 World Bible Translation Center.

Scripture taken from the New King James Version®. Copyright © 1982 by Thomas Nelson, Inc. Used by permission. All rights reserved.

THE HOLY BIBLE, NEW INTERNATIONAL VERSION®, NIV® Copyright © 1973, 1978, 1984, 2011 by Biblica, Inc.™ Used by permission. All rights reserved worldwide.

Scripture quotations marked (NLT) are taken from the Holy Bible, New Living Translation,

Copyright and Fair-use

copyright © 1996, 2004, v 2007 by Tyndale House Foundation. Used by permission of Tyndale House Publishers, Inc., Carol Stream, IL 60188. All rights reserved.

Scriptures marked NLV are taken from the New Life Version. Used by permission. © Christian Literature International. All rights reserved.

Scriptures marked TLB are taken from the THE LIVING BIBLE (TLB): Scripture taken from THE LIVING BIBLE copyright© 1971. Used by permission of Tyndale House Publishers, Inc., Carol Stream, Illinois 60188. All rights reserved.

Scriptures marked VOICE are taken from The Voice™. Copyright © 2008 by Ecclesia Bible Society. Used by permission. All rights reserved.

You will find them on almost every page.

Dedication

I dedicate this book to the Love of my life, God. He has been with me all the days of my life, He encourages me, strengthens me, prospers me, and shows me His love in new ways all the time. I am supremely blessed to know Love that surpasses all knowledge. Thank You, Father, Son and Holy Spirit for pouring love into me!

Dedicate yourself to being loved by God.

Table of Contents

ii. Copyright and Fair-use

iv. Dedication

v. Table of Contents

vii. God Woos Us

ix. Foreword

1. In the Beginning Was Love

11. Love's Identity

25. Are We Deserving of Love?

33. Love's Adoption Agent

43. Love's Reward

49. Love Values Us

59. Never-ending Love

67. The Love Chapter: 1 Cor. 13

85. Taste and See Love

97. Love Walk

105. Partner with Love

God loves you unconditionally.

Table of Contents

113. Love Cleanses Lepers

117. Sowing and Reaping in Love

125. Love Like Jesus

147. Love Forgives

171. My Love Testimonies

185. Love Gives Gifts

B. My Prayer for You

J. About the Author

O. Get in Touch

N. Search for Love

God is watching over you in love.

God Woos Us

We are born into a world of sin. God, since the Fall of Man, has been trying to convince His creation to love Him. Since we have been born, God has been loving us, sending messengers with His telegrams, and personally calling our names.

He is wooing us. We are the desire of His affection. It is a challenge, but God is infinitely creative. He enjoys wooing us to Him. He wants to move us away from the darkness and into light: the perfect light of His love. God has fun displaying Love to all!

We are His unique Love story. Those He wins are treasured and given His full attention. He is so enamored and interested in each of us! Otherwise, He wouldn't have pursued us so fiercely. He would not have sent Jesus if He saw us as nothing. He is always sharing with us, blessing us, and talking with us.

God has an awesome journey planned while we are here. He will provide everything you will need here to meet His vision for your life, which is better than we can even think! A part of Heaven is designed for you. He is learning what you like in this life so He can completely exceed your

Love enjoys spending time with you.

expectations when you get to Heaven! That's the kind of lover our God is: the Ultimate Lover!

Throughout this book we will dive into the different aspects of Love. God is infinite; there's always more to learn about Him! Even when we experience eternity we won't ever stop learning about Love! Buckle in, grab a drink, cozy up to a nice comfortable spot, and feast on the Love of God as you read this book.

Invite God to take part in life with you.

Foreword

I count it a privilege and an honor to share the foreword of this awesome and amazing love letter, "God: The Ultimate Lover." He established this whole universe in Love, through Love, and to be Love. For God so loved the world that He gave His Love that whosoever believes in His Love shall not perish but have everlasting life.

I believe that if anyone gets the true revelation of His love then they will see with new lens the purpose of life and living. Recently, the Holy Spirit told me that the gift you receive is the gift that you become. I believe this to be our primary purpose. Not to build our own ministry or to follow destiny but I believe it is for us to portray an accurate reflection of the love of God in the image of His Son, Jesus Christ, Our Lord and Savior: the true Gift of Love.

Aaron Beach, my friend, brother, and co-laborer in the Gospel has captured the true image of the ultimate love that comes from our Father. Not just in words but also in deeds and acts of kindness. Aaron is a gentle, kind, loving, humble, and patient expression of God's love.

Love is writing a perfect story through your life.

Foreword

My prayer is that you receive the full measure of His love through this brilliant body of work. So, let your heart be open to the precious flow of the Holy Spirit to imprint on your heart the truth of His love.

Stephanie Turner,
Pastor of Love Life Ministries

Love changes lives around in an instant.

God: The Ultimate Lover

CHAPTER 2

In the Beginning Was Love

> **John 1:1 KJV —** 1 In the beginning was the Word, and the Word was with God, and the Word was God.

God existed before creating our universe. He has always been and always will be. God is Love. Love encompasses all the qualities of God. He spoke all the universe to being through love. The universe is constantly expanding: following the creative word of Love that made it.

The spoken Word of Love is still holding everything in the physical realm together. Scientists still do not know what keeps protons, neutrons, and electrons from crashing into each other. They have no clue what force keeps them equidistant and leads them along invisible paths that never cross. The quantum realm is full of mysteries that make no sense to natural laws, but we have inside knowledge; Love is sustaining all existence.

> **Colossians 1:17 NLT —** 17 He existed before anything else, and He holds all creation together.

> **1 John 4:16 NLT —** 16 We know how much God loves us, and we have put our trust in His love.

 You are the object of the Father's loving desire.

In the Beginning Was Love

> God is Love, and all who live in love live in God, and God lives in them.

Love is who God is. It is the same love that the Trinity shares. The Father enjoys such a perfect love relationship with Christ and Holy Spirit that He wanted to share it with a like-minded being made in His image. God wanted a family to love, bless, and to enjoy fellowship.

John 17:24 NLT — 24 Father, I want these whom You have given Me to be with Me where I am. Then they can see all the glory You gave Me because You loved Me even before the world began!

Genesis 1:26-27 NIV — 26 Then God said, "Let Us make mankind in Our image, in Our likeness, so that they may rule over the fish in the sea and the birds in the sky, over the livestock and all the wild animals, and over all the creatures that move along the ground." 27 So God created mankind in His Own image, in the image of God He created them; male and female He created them.

Everything began with the Word of Love! Love

God is speaking love over you.

In the Beginning Was Love

inspired God to create us. God gave the Earth to humankind to care for. He created the universe for us to enjoy together. It is our playground. It is filled with all sorts of wonders for us to discover together. It is part of our inheritance.

> **Hebrews 1:2 NLT** — 2 And now in these final days, He has spoken to us through His Son. God promised everything to the Son as an inheritance, and through the Son He created the universe.

We were created to share life with God. He designed all of creation with a focus on how much we would enjoy it with Him. All mountains, forests, caves, bodies of water, and biomes show off the creativity of God. They point us to admire the majesty of our awesome God.

> **Isaiah 55:12 NLV** — 12 You will go out with joy, and be led out in peace. The mountains and the hills will break out into sounds of joy before you. And all the trees of the field will clap their hands.

Out of everything He has created, we were the only ones made like Him. We were created to be

You are invaluable to Love.

In the Beginning Was Love

filled with God's love. He made us to propagate His love throughout the universe. Love enjoys creating new things. We are able, through Love, to create things in joy like Him! God had fun creating our universe! Creativity was given to us as a primary way to be like our Father!

The details of a single flower for example, all the wrinkles, colorations, and symmetrical linework come together in grandiose harmony. The fragrance it produces draws bees to pollinate it and then they use that pollen to make sweet honey. Nature works together perfectly because God creatively designed it to be beautiful from the start and yet God loves humankind more.

> **Matthew 6:30 TLB** — 30 And if God cares so wonderfully for flowers that are here today and gone tomorrow, won't He more surely care for you, O men of little faith?

God set us above all else on Earth to tend, care for, and watch over the plants and animals.

> **Genesis 1:28 CSB** — 28 God blessed them, and God said to them, "Be fruitful, multiply, fill the earth, and subdue it. Rule the fish of the sea, the

You have the authority to rule in Love.

In the Beginning Was Love

birds of the sky, and every creature that crawls on the earth."

There are many instances of animals asking humans for help when they get in trouble. I remember watching a video about a baby elephant rescue. A baby elephant fell into a muddy hole. It tried for hours to get out and could not. The herd of elephants tried to pull it up and could not reach it. The baby elephant was getting weary and beginning to sink further down. The elephants began trumpeting in a panic! A guy driving by heard the trumpeting and drove close to see what was going on. The elephants approached him in a frenzy and attempted to guide him somewhere. He got the hint and followed them and they showed him where the baby elephant was trapped.

He took out his phone and called help over. They brought in construction equipment to dig out a ramp for the baby elephant. The herd quieted down when they saw that the humans were doing what they could to help. They looked on as the process took hours into the night. Once the baby elephant was able to get out and was

Love needs you in this world..

joined with the herd again, the elephants bowed their heads to the humans that helped them and also trumpeted a different tune to thank them. We have dominion over all creatures! They know that we are God's representatives.

> **Romans 8:19-21 TLB —** 19 For all creation is waiting patiently and hopefully for that future day when God will resurrect His children. 20-21 For on that day thorns and thistles, sin, death, and decay—the things that overcame the world against its will at God's command—will all disappear, and the world around us will share in the glorious freedom from sin which God's children enjoy.

We have been given so much more than just dominion over animals though! Love has provided everything we will ever need. Adam and Eve had all their needs met through God's provision. He prepared for their arrival. He planted a Garden in Eden that contained all types of fruit and vegetables to eat. They had animals to watch over. They had an idyllic paradise to explore. Who knows what kind of wonders they had access to? It was the perfect place for them.

All of Love's promises are Yes & Amen.

In the Beginning Was Love

Love set up their identity. Love blessed them to prosper. Love gave them meaning and purpose for their lives. It is the same with us! God has prepared ahead of time the paths of righteousness of which we would walk.

> **Jeremiah 29:11 CSB —** 11 "For I know the plans I have for you" -- this is the LORD's declaration -- "plans for your well-being, not for disaster, to give you a future and a hope.
>
> **Romans 9:23 YLT —** 23 and that He might make known the riches of His glory on vessels of kindness, that He before prepared for glory, whom also He did call -- us --
>
> **Psalm 23:3 VOICE —** 3 He makes me whole again, steering me off worn, hard paths to roads where truth and righteousness echo His name.

Love has blessed us with every spiritual blessing and every need is met through boundless grace.

> **Ephesians 1:3 CSB —** 3 Blessed is the God and Father of our Lord Jesus Christ, who has blessed us with every spiritual blessing in the heavens in Christ

Receive of God's bountiful love.

In the Beginning Was Love

> **2 Peter 1:3 VOICE** — 3 His divine power has given us everything we need to experience life and to reflect God's true nature through the knowledge of the One who called us by His glory and virtue.

Praise the Lord for His faithful love towards us! God's entire existence is for you! The entirety of God is toward you and it is all love!

 Love abounds in goodness and grace toward your life.

CHAPTER 2

Love's Identity

God identifies Himself as Love. It is the way He relates to us. It is who He is. He cannot be anything else. God only is Love. Love labels everything that God is, and because that is who He is, His actions are always born of love.

> **1 John 4:9 ERV** — 9 This is how God showed His love to us: He sent His only Son into the world to give us life through Him.

Everything in the universe responds to Love because it was created in Love: plants grow better, animals behave, humans accomplish more, rocks roll away, land yields more, and skies clear out. We all desire love; the kind of love that only God can give. We are built up, exhorted, encouraged, and motivated by actions of Love. Jesus demonstrated what Love looks like. We follow His example!

> **John 5:19 ERV** — 19 But Jesus answered, "I assure you that the Son can do nothing alone. He does only what He sees His Father doing. The Son does the same things that the Father does.

Love is logical. Love makes good decisions. Love is not irrational and Love is not crazy. Love is a choice to value the other party no matter what.

 Love thinks about you and smiles.

Everyone wants love. We were created to need Love. God is Love and He only makes good decisions. Jesus said the whole of the law can be summed up in two commandments; love God and love people the same way He does.

> **Matthew 22:37 NIV** — 37 Jesus replied: " 'Love the Lord your God with all your heart and with all your soul and with all your mind.'
>
> **John 15:12 NLV** — 12 This is what I tell you to do: Love each other just as I have loved you.

Jesus' life is based in Love. Love propelled Him to heal the sick, cast out devils, raise the dead, and cleanse lepers. Love compelled Him to take the punishment of the cross for us. Love makes sense. Love describes why we are here. Love is the purpose for every created thing. Love truly does make the world go around.

> **Mark 1:41 NLT** — 41 Moved with compassion, Jesus reached out and touched him. "I am willing," He said. "Be healed!"
>
> **Acts 10:38 VOICE** — 38 You know God identified Jesus as the uniquely chosen One by pouring out the Holy Spirit on Him, by empowering Him.

Love compels you to make a positive difference.

Love's Identity

> You know Jesus went through the land doing good for all and healing all who were suffering under the oppression of the evil one, for God was with Him.

Love is not a feeling or emotion. Love is a choice. Love is a verb. It is an outward action resulting in goodwill toward another: to put someone else's needs ahead of your own. Jesus had a choice; He was not forced into accepting the cross, but He made the choice for us.

> **Luke 22:41-44 TLB** — 41-42 He walked away, perhaps a stone's throw, and knelt down and prayed this prayer: "Father, if You are willing, please take away this cup of horror from Me. But I want Your will, not Mine." 43 Then an angel from heaven appeared and strengthened Him, 44 for He was in such agony of spirit that He broke into a sweat of blood, with great drops falling to the ground as He prayed more and more earnestly.

Love compels action. I daresay Love will always lead to action. The greatest love is sacrificial love: choosing another's life over your

Jesus is glad you chose Him.

own. Jesus experienced this firsthand, He sacrificed His life for you and me. He chose us over Himself.

> **John 15:13 NLV —** 13 No one can have greater love than to give his life for his friends.

Jesus' life on earth was modeled after Love. He had compassion on those who were unwell or afflicted and He fervently desired to heal them all, and heal them all He did. He saw them as lost sheep and He was the Good Shepherd. Shepherds watch out for their flock. They nurture, protect, care for, feed, and monitor each of their sheep. They lead them along safe paths. Sheep trust their shepherds. What a great image of our Savior!

> **Mark 6:34 NLT —** 34 Jesus saw the huge crowd as He stepped from the boat, and He had compassion on them because they were like sheep without a shepherd. So He began teaching them many things.
>
> **John 10:11 TLB —** 11 I am the Good Shepherd. The Good Shepherd lays down His life for the sheep.

You can hear God's voice of love.

Love's Identity

Jesus took our dirty rags and gave us His own righteousness. It is called the Great Exchange because He took on our fallen nature and we took on His divine righteousness.

> **Romans 3:23 VOICE** — 23 You see, all have sinned, and all their futile attempts to reach God in His glory fail.

> **Isaiah 1:18 TLB** — 18 Come, let's talk this over, says the Lord; no matter how deep the stain of your sins, I can take it out and make you as clean as freshly fallen snow. Even if you are stained as red as crimson, I can make you white as wool!

Look at all the death Jesus suffered through to give us His life!

Jesus was despised so we could be loved.

> **Luke 23:34-37 NKJV** — 34 Then Jesus said, "Father, forgive them, for they do not know what they do." And they divided His garments and cast lots. 35 And the people stood looking on. But even the rulers with them sneered, saying, "He saved others; let Him save Himself if

Love conquered death for you.

He is the Christ, the chosen of God." 36 The soldiers also mocked Him, coming and offering Him sour wine, 37 and saying, "If You are the King of the Jews, save Yourself."

Jesus was bruised and hurt so we could be healed.

Isaiah 53:3-5 NLV — 3 He was hated and men would have nothing to do with Him, a man of sorrow and suffering, knowing sadness well. We hid, as it were, our faces from Him. He was hated, and we did not think well of Him. 4 For sure He took on Himself our troubles and carried our sorrows. Yet we thought of Him as being punished and hurt by God, and made to suffer. 5 But He was hurt for our wrong-doing. He was crushed for our sins. He was punished so we would have peace. He was beaten so we would be healed.

1 Peter 2:24 TLB — 24 He personally carried the load of our sins in His own body when He died on the cross so that we can be finished with sin and live a good life from now on. For His wounds have healed ours!

Love erased the curse of the law.

Jesus was cursed so we could be blessed.

> **Galatians 3:13-14 ERV** — 13 The law says we are under a curse for not always obeying it. But Christ took away that curse. He changed places with us and put Himself under that curse. The Scriptures say, "Anyone who is hung on a tree is under a curse." 14 Because of what Jesus Christ did, the blessing God promised to Abraham was given to all people. Christ died so that by believing in Him we could have the Spirit that God promised.

Jesus became poor (restriction of divinity by taking on mankind's identity) so we could be made rich.

> **2 Corinthians 8:9 VOICE** — 9 You know the grace that has come to us through our Lord Jesus the Anointed. He set aside His infinite riches and was born into the lowest circumstance so that you may gain great riches through His humble poverty.

Jesus was made to be an offering for sin so we could be made the righteousness of God.

 Love has made you righteous.

2 Corinthians 5:21 VOICE — 21 He orchestrated this: the Anointed One, who had never experienced sin, became sin for us so that in Him we might embody the very righteousness of God.

Jesus was forsaken so we would never be left alone.

Mark 15:34 ERV — 34 At three o'clock Jesus cried out loudly, "Eloi, Eloi, lama sabachthani." This means "My God, my God, why have You left Me alone?"

Jesus subjugated His authority so we could have all authority.

Matthew 28:18 NKJV — 18 And Jesus came and spoke to them, saying, "All authority has been given to Me in heaven and on earth.

Colossians 1:15-16 VOICE — 15 He is the exact image of the invisible God, the firstborn of creation, the eternal. 16 It was by Him that everything was created: the heavens, the earth, all things within and upon them, all things seen and unseen, thrones and dominions, spiritual

Love has given you victory.

Love's Identity

powers and authorities. Every detail was crafted through His design, by His own hands, and for His purposes.

Jesus tasted death so we could partake of life.

Hebrews 2:9 ERV — 9 For a short time Jesus was made lower than the angels, but now we see Him wearing a crown of glory and honor because He suffered and died. Because of God's grace, Jesus died for everyone.

Romans 5:17-18 VOICE — 17 If one man's sin brought a reign of death—that's Adam's legacy—how much more will those who receive grace in abundance and the free gift of redeeming justice reign in life by means of one other Man—Jesus the Anointed. 18 So here is the result: as one man's sin brought about condemnation and punishment for all people, so one Man's act of faithfulness makes all of us right with God and brings us to new life.

Jesus was thrown into chaos so we could have peace.

 Love has provided peace to your heart.

Luke 22:44 TLB — 44 for He was in such agony of spirit that He broke into a sweat of blood, with great drops falling to the ground as He prayed more and more earnestly.

Romans 5:1 NLV — 1 Now that we have been made right with God by putting our trust in Him, we have peace with Him. It is because of what our Lord Jesus Christ did for us.

Jesus became the object of scorn so we could become adopted sons and daughters.

Romans 8:15-17 VOICE — 15 You see, you have not received a spirit that returns you to slavery, so you have nothing to fear. The Spirit you have received adopts you and welcomes you into God's own family. That's why we call out to Him, "Abba! Father!" as we would address a loving daddy. 16 Through that prayer, God's Spirit confirms in our spirits that we are His children. 17 If we are God's children, that means we are His heirs along with the Anointed, set to inherit everything that is His. If we share His sufferings, we know that we will ultimately share in His glory.

Love has welcomed you into His family.

Love's Identity

Galatians 3:26 NLV — 26 You are now children of God because you have put your trust in Christ Jesus.

Jesus took all judgment on Himself so we would not have to be judged.

1 John 4:17 TLB — 17 And as we live with Christ, our love grows more perfect and complete; so we will not be ashamed and embarrassed at the day of judgment, but can face Him with confidence and joy because He loves us and we love Him too.

Romans 5:8-10 TLB — 8 But God showed His great love for us by sending Christ to die for us while we were still sinners. 9 And since by His blood He did all this for us as sinners, how much more will He do for us now that He has declared us not guilty? Now He will save us from all of God's wrath to come. 10 And since, when we were His enemies, we were brought back to God by the death of His Son, what blessings He must have for us now that we are His friends and He is living within us!

Love removed all condemnation.

Christ Jesus is the exact representation of God the Father; an image of Love!

> **John 14:10-11 NLT —** 10 Don't you believe that I AM in the Father and the Father is in Me? The words I speak are not My own, but my Father who lives in Me does His work through Me. 11 Just believe that I AM in the Father and the Father is in Me. Or at least believe because of the work you have seen Me do.
>
> **John 15:9 TLB —** 9 I have loved you even as the Father has loved Me. Live within My love.
>
> **John 16:27-28 ERV —** 27 The Father Himself loves you because you have loved Me. And He loves you because you have believed that I came from God. 28 I came from the Father into the world. Now I AM leaving the world and going back to the Father."

Praise Jesus for showing us the identity of the Father which is all love!

Love defines your true identity.

about you.

CHAPTER 8

Are We Deserving of Love?

Have you ever heard the question or statement, "Are we deserving of God's love?" I have heard it countless times in songs and doctrines. What does this mean though? How can we understand the answer from a Biblical standpoint? Let us first start with a definition of, 'deserve.'

> To merit, be qualified for, or have a claim to (reward, assistance, punishment, etc.) because of actions, qualities, or situation

Let us break this statement down using our theological understanding.

Are we of merit or are we qualified because of what we have done? Does what we do effect the love of God in anyway? A resounding... nope! We cannot earn Love by works. Paul talks profusely about this in Galatians.

> **Galatians 3:1 TLB —** 1 Oh, foolish Galatians! What magician has hypnotized you and cast an evil spell upon you? For you used to see the meaning of Jesus Christ's death as clearly as though I had waved a placard before you with a picture on it of Christ dying on the cross.

 We could not earn it but He gave Love freely.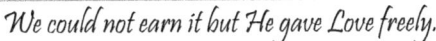

Are We Deserving of Love?

> **Galatians 5:1 VOICE** — 1 So stand strong for our freedom! The Anointed One freed us so we wouldn't spend one more day under the yoke of slavery, trapped under the law.

The Galatians' church was led astray by leaders saying to stay saved in Jesus they needed to become circumcised and follow the Old Testament laws. Paul vehemently and passionately spoke against that mindset in his scathing Galatians epistle. No you cannot mix faith and law; it will never work! Jesus superseded the law by fulfilling it perfectly in the flesh thereby erasing all of the requirements for us.

> **Hebrews 8:6 ERV** — 6 But the work that has been given to Jesus is much greater than the work that was given to those priests. In the same way, the new agreement that Jesus brought from God to His people is much greater than the old one. And the new agreement is based on better promises.

> **Galatians 3:13 NLT** — 13 But Christ has rescued us from the curse pronounced by the law. When He was hung on the cross, He took upon Himself

Faith gives us access to Love's promises.

the curse for our wrongdoing. For it is written in the Scriptures, "Cursed is everyone who is hung on a tree."

We can never get Love by working for it. Love cannot be earned. God's love is unconditional meaning we cannot affect it.

Are we loved by God because of who we are? I believe God loves the whole of His creation. We are uniquely created in His image but that is not the only reason God loves us. We are also unholy by the sin nature that we inherited from Adam; God has no place for the unholy.

> **Genesis 3:22-24 ERV —** 22 The Lord God said, "Look, the man has become like Us—he knows about good and evil. And now the man might take the fruit from the tree of life. If the man eats that fruit, he will live forever." 23 So the Lord God forced the man out of the Garden of Eden to work the ground he was made from. 24 God forced the man to leave the garden. Then He put Cherub angels and a sword of fire at the entrance to the garden to protect it. The sword flashed around and around, guarding the way to the tree of life.

God loves us just as we are.

Are We Deserving of Love?

God is holy and cannot associate with things that are not. It is part of what makes God... GOD. He is holy (set apart) from all else.

> **Hebrews 7:26 VOICE** — 26 It is only fitting that we should have a High Priest who is devoted to God, blameless, pure, compassionate toward but separate from sinners, and exalted by God to the highest place of honor..

So, no we are not loved by God just because we were made in His image. He loves everything He has created. Unconditional love cannot be manipulated.

What about our situations? Does God love us because we were unable to pull ourselves out of sin? God always planned to send Jesus to save us. Mankind would never be able to sustain their own salvation, but God does not just love us because we cannot save ourselves. He knew that Jesus would come through and bring all His followers into Heaven. Unconditional love cannot be changed.

> **Colossians 1:22 NLV** — 22 But Christ has brought you back to God by His death on the cross. In

Sin can never stop Love.

Are We Deserving of Love?

this way, Christ can bring you to God, holy and pure and without blame.

To summarize, no we are not deserving of God's love since that would be an attribute that would affect the unconditional status of Love. Now, let us look at it from a different point-of-view. Did Adam and Eve deserve God's love even before the fall?

Does a child deserve love from their parents? No! However, I believe there is an innate responsibility to take care of one's own. God put that desire in us. I believe He has the same desire. He has a self-proclaimed responsibility to take care of His own creation made in His image. A child does not earn love from their parents. The parents simply love their child because they are theirs. It is the parents' choice.

> **Matthew 7:9-11 VOICE —** 9 Think of it this way: if your son asked you for bread, would you give him a stone? Of course not—you would give him a loaf of bread. 10 If your son asked for a fish, would you give him a snake? No, to be sure, you would give him a fish—the best fish you could find. 11 So if you, who are sinful, know how to

 God knows how to love and bless His kids.

give your children good gifts, how much more so does your Father in heaven, who is perfect, know how to give great gifts to His children!

The child has no say in the matter. We have no say in the matter. God has told us He is Love and we must accept that as truth. He has chosen to love us through the redeeming power of Christ. We can do nothing to earn God's love, we can do nothing to lose it, and we can do nothing to affect the outcome. His love is a constant and unchanging force. We are His own and He has taken us on as His responsibility to love.

We do not deserve God's love, but He has CHOSEN to lavish it on us!

> **1 Thessalonians 1:4 ERV** — 4 Brothers and sisters, God loves you. And we know that He has chosen you to be His people.

> **Psalm 31:19 NLT** — 19 How great is the goodness You have stored up for those who fear You. You lavish it on those who come to You for protection, blessing them before the watching world.

We are chosen by Love to be love.

I have been watching

CHAPTER 4

Love's Adoption Agent

We are born into this world estranged from God because of Adam's sin. We are not able to know Him fully. Satan is the usurper. He took the place of God in our lives through humankind's indiscretion. He is holding us back from knowing our true Father. Satan is an abusive father. He steals, kills, and destroys those under his authority.

> **John 10:10 NKJV** — 10 "The thief does not come except to steal, and to kill, and to destroy. I have come that they may have life, and that they may have it more abundantly.

Satan stole us away from the Father. Satan is the father of lies. He wants to hold on to us as long as he can just so God cannot have us. What a wicked fiend Satan is!

> **John 8:44 VOICE** — 44 You are just like your true father, the devil; and you spend your time pursuing the things your father loves. He started out as a killer, and he cannot tolerate truth because he is void of anything true. At the core of his character, he is a liar; everything he speaks originates in these lies because he is the father of lies.

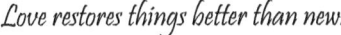

Love restores things better than new.

However, God had a plan to restore us!

> **Romans 3:25-26 ERV** — 25-26 God gave Jesus as a way to forgive people's sins through their faith in Him. God can forgive them because the blood sacrifice of Jesus pays for their sins. God gave Jesus to show that He always does what is right and fair. He was right in the past when He was patient and did not punish people for their sins. And in our own time He still does what is right. God worked all this out in a way that allows Him to judge people fairly and still make right any person who has faith in Jesus.
>
> **Romans 5:17 VOICE** — 17 If one man's sin brought a reign of death—that's Adam's legacy—how much more will those who receive grace in abundance and the free gift of redeeming justice reign in life by means of one other Man—Jesus the Anointed.

It did not surprise God that humankind could not maintain their righteousness in their own strength. Humankind needed a Savior even before they were created. God's first plan and best plan was to send Jesus. He sent Jesus before the foundation of the world, to rescue us from

God sent Love (Jesus) to save you.

Love's Adoption Agent

ourselves and Satan.

> **Hebrews 9:26 TLB** — 26 If that had been necessary, then He would have had to die again and again, ever since the world began. But no! He came once for all, at the end of the age, to put away the power of sin forever by dying for us.

Satan deceived us and stole everything that defined us. Jesus came to restore everything Satan stole plus to give us authority to trump him.

> **Ephesians 1:18-22 VOICE** — 18 Open the eyes of their hearts, and let the light of Your truth flood in. Shine Your light on the hope You are calling them to embrace. Reveal to them the glorious riches You are preparing as their inheritance. 19 Let them see the full extent of Your power that is at work in those of us who believe, and may it be done according to Your might and power. Friends, it is this same might and resurrection power that 20 He used in the Anointed One to raise Him from the dead and to position Him at His right hand in heaven. There is nothing over Him. 21 He's above all rule, authority, power, and dominion; over

Love always provides in abundance.

every name invoked, over every title bestowed in this age and the next. 22 God has placed all things beneath His feet and anointed Him as the head over all things for His church.

Jesus became the adoption agent who has been given all authority as humankind's representative to reclaim the Father's children from the terrible father. He had the approval of God and humankind. Jesus as a sinless Man, kept every part of the Old Testament covenant thereby giving Him access to all the benefits of the blessings of God.

> **Galatians 3:14 NLT —** 14 Through Christ Jesus, God has blessed the Gentiles with the same blessing He promised to Abraham, so that we who are believers might receive the promised Holy Spirit through faith.

On top of that, death could find no fault in Him due to His sinless nature. He arose from the Grave with all authority in His hands. Jesus defeated Satan in a complete one-sided conquest. Now, Satan has no legal right to those who have chosen Jesus as their Lord and Savior.

Love resurrects dead things to life.

Love's Adoption Agent

Colossians 2:13-15 TLB — 13 You were dead in sins, and your sinful desires were not yet cut away. Then He gave you a share in the very life of Christ, for He forgave all your sins, 14 and blotted out the charges proved against you, the list of His commandments which you had not obeyed. He took this list of sins and destroyed it by nailing it to Christ's cross. 15 In this way God took away Satan's power to accuse you of sin, and God openly displayed to the whole world Christ's triumph at the cross where your sins were all taken away.

Matthew 28:18-20 ERV — 18 So He came to them and said, "All authority in heaven and on earth is given to Me. 19 So go and make followers of all people in the world. Baptize them in the name of the Father and the Son and the Holy Spirit. 20 Teach them to obey everything that I have told you to do. You can be sure that I will be with you always. I will continue with you until the end of time.

Satan still keeps people in the dark. He does not want the world to know he is defeated, and is now wrongfully keeping God's children from Him.

God alights Himself through Love.

> **2 Corinthians 4:4 ERV** — 4 The ruler of this world has blinded the minds of those who don't believe. They cannot see the light of the Good News—the message about the divine greatness of Christ. Christ is the One who is exactly like God.

However, Jesus raised up disciples to share His victory with any who will believe. He sent Holy Spirit to His followers to make them witnesses. They demonstrated through signs, wonders, and miracles the love of Jesus. They also sought out to destroy all the workings of Satan and his kingdom's influence.

> **Acts 1:8 VOICE** — 8 Here's the knowledge you need: you will receive power when the Holy Spirit comes on you. And you will be My witnesses, first here in Jerusalem, then beyond to Judea and Samaria, and finally to the farthest places on earth.
>
> **Acts 10:38-41 VOICE** — 38 You know God identified Jesus as the uniquely chosen One by pouring out the Holy Spirit on Him, by empowering Him. You know Jesus went through the land doing good for all and healing all who were suffering under the oppression of the evil

Love flows through us to bless others.

Love's Adoption Agent

one, for God was with Him. 39 My friends and I stand as witnesses to all Jesus did in the region of Judea and the city of Jerusalem. The people of our capital city killed Him by hanging Him on a tree, 40 but God raised Him up on the third day and made it possible for us to see Him. 41 Not everyone was granted this privilege, only those of us whom God chose as witnesses. We actually ate and drank with Him after His resurrection.

When a child becomes of decision age, they can choose to know their other parent. The time of decision is now! Jesus has given all humanity the right to choose to Him. We can help our future brothers and sisters see how awesome their true Father is: how much better He treats His own, how much He cares for them, and how He provides for His own. When they see the goodness of God, they cannot help but be drawn to His grace and love; they will choose to know Love!

> Romans 2:4 TLB — 4 Don't you realize how patient He is being with you? Or don't you care? Can't you see that He has been waiting all this

We choose to know Love.

time without punishing you, to give you time to turn from your sin? His kindness is meant to lead you to repentance."

Matthew 5:14 NKJV — 14 You are the light of the world. A city that is set on a hill cannot be hidden.

The world needs help that only God can provide. We can stand up and shine the light of the truth of God's Word to the masses. We can be the agents of change that show a dying world the love of the Father!

Be the image of Love to the world.

CHAPTER 9

Love's Reward

Love works hard. Have you ever thought... who labored harder than Jesus?

1 Timothy 5:18 ERV — 18 As the Scriptures say, "When a work animal is being used to separate grain, don't keep it from eating the grain." And the Scriptures also say, "A worker should be given his pay."

Jesus is worthy of His reward! But what did He choose? What could an Almighty God desire?

John 17:9-10, 19-21 VOICE — 9 I am now making an appeal to You on their behalf. This request is not for the entire world; it is for those whom You have given to Me because they are Yours. 10 Yours and Mine, Mine and Yours, for all that are Mine are Yours. Through them I have been glorified.. ... 19 It is entirely for their benefit that I have set Myself apart so that they may be set apart by truth. 20 I am not asking solely for their benefit; this prayer is also for all the believers who will follow them and hear them speak. 21 Father, may they all be one as You are in Me and I am in You; may they be in Us, for by this unity the world will believe that You sent Me.

He chose us! He chose to have a relationship

Love desires relationship with others.

with us as His reward! He chose to adopt us into His family.

> **Ephesians 1:5 TLB** — 5 His unchanging plan has always been to adopt us into His own family by sending Jesus Christ to die for us. And He did this because He wanted to!

Jesus worked hard for us. He did not want anyone to perish: including Judas but that was prophesied ahead of time. He was pushed beyond His body's limits and found His strength in the Father. He was persecuted, betrayed by the ones He loved, wrongly accused, tortured, and then abandoned by the Father if only for a moment that must have felt like an eternity. And yet, He would do it all over again for you to know how much He loves you.

> **Hebrews 12:2 NLT** — 2 ...Because of the joy awaiting Him, He endured the cross, disregarding its shame. Now He is seated in the place of honor beside God's throne.

He conquered death for us to have life. He released Holy Spirit to empower us with the same strength He had to minister and love. Who

Jesus worked hard to win your heart.

Love's Reward

worked harder than Jesus? Who will labor with Jesus to bring in the harvest? Who will stand up in His name? Who will carry His love to the ends of the Earth?

> **Romans 10:13-15 TLB —** 13 Anyone who calls upon the name of the Lord will be saved. 14 But how shall they ask Him to save them unless they believe in Him? And how can they believe in Him if they have never heard about Him? And how can they hear about Him unless someone tells them? 15 And how will anyone go and tell them unless someone sends him? That is what the Scriptures are talking about when they say, "How beautiful are the feet of those who preach the Gospel of peace with God and bring glad tidings of good things." In other words, how welcome are those who come preaching God's Good News!

It is us! We're the ones He has sent. He has called us by His name. He identifies with us and we with Him. Through the power of Holy Spirit we are co-laborers with Christ that are well able to bring in the harvest.

> **1 Corinthians 3:8 ERV —** 8 The one who plants

We rest in Love and release all stress.

and the one who waters have the same purpose. And each one will be rewarded for his own work.

Matthew 10:1 VOICE — 1 Jesus called His twelve disciples to Him. He endowed them with the authority to heal sickness and disease and to drive demons out of those who were possessed.

He showed us the works of righteousness that come from a pure relationship with God the Father. He healed multitudes of people. He traveled all over and taught countless curious folk the ways of His kingdom. Who worked harder than Jesus? And yet, He did it all to show His immense love for people. What an awesome Savior! Let us imitate Him like innocent children and share His love with all.

Matthew 11:28-30 ERV — 28 "Come to Me all of you who are tired from the heavy burden you have been forced to carry. I will give you rest. 29 Accept My teaching. Learn from Me. I am gentle and humble in spirit. And you will be able to get some rest. 30 Yes, the teaching that I ask you to accept is easy. The load I give you to carry is light."

We work through Love.

Love's Reward

Ephesians 5:1 TLB — 1 Follow God's example in everything you do just as a much loved child imitates his father.

We imitate our Father to love like Him.

CHAPTER 8
Love Values Us

Love has established our true worth. In the example below, I am going to use coin collecting as a way to show you how much God values His children.

Coins are composed of precious metals. God made all the metals, materials of the Earth, land biomes, and gemstones when He spoke land into existence. Later on, He fearfully and wonderfully made us from the dust of the Earth: the components of the land.

> **Psalm 139:16-18 VOICE** — 16 You see all things; You saw me growing, changing in my mother's womb; Every detail of my life was already written in Your book; You established the length of my life before I ever tasted the sweetness of it. 17 Your thoughts and plans are treasures to me, O God! I cherish each and every one of them! How grand in scope! How many in number! 18 If I could count each one of them, they would be more than all the grains of sand on earth. Their number is inconceivable! Even when I wake up, I am still near to You.

We have humble beginnings but we were created for a purpose.

> **Jeremiah 29:11 CSB** — 11 "For I know the plans I

God exchanged His Son for your precious life.

> have for you" -- this is the LORD's declaration -- "plans for your well-being, not for disaster, to give you a future and a hope.

Soil is powerful. When seeds are planted into good soil and tended, a harvest ensues. We are like living soil. We plant seeds of good (or bad) in our heart (through words, thoughts, and actions) and we get a harvest. We were created to establish the Kingdom of Heaven on Earth: to share the love of God with every created thing.

> **Mark 16:15 NKJV —** 15 And He said to them, "Go into all the world and preach the gospel to every creature.

Have you ever noticed that there are so many different types of coins? There are an innumerable amount of coins with varying designs, storied origins, and rich histories. Each coin is uniquely made. Even in the same press there are micro differences unseen by the eye. They have been to and fro throughout the Earth as each one has passed through an untold amount of human hands, treasuries, and banks. The plethora of

---

You are uniquely blessed by Love to love others.

Love Values Us

transactions each coin has been through must be staggering. If coins could talk they would have much to say. In the same way, we are each created uniquely by the Father. Every time He knits another baby together in the womb: He breaks the mold. Even identical twins that share the same genetic code are not the same person. Each person has a good purpose designed by a loving Father. He gifts each person with varying talents and abilities to accomplish His purpose in their life.

> **1 Peter 4:10 ERV** — 10 God has shown you His grace in many different ways. So be good servants and use whatever gift He has given you in a way that will best serve each other..

To anyone who sees a coin they can see the value. Pennies are worth one cent. Nickels are worth five cents. Quarters are worth twenty-five cents and so on. There are many types of coins with varying values, but to a collector, the coin is worth the price they are willing to pay. To you a penny could be worth one cent but to a collector that specific penny could be worth thousands.

Your life is important to God.

Love Values Us

The collector sets the value of the coin regardless of the face value. We can see how much God values us based on the price He was willing to pay. What would you value Jesus' life at? How much is He worth? Because that is what the Father paid to have claim to you. We cannot fathom how much God values us!

> **1 Corinthians 6:20 NLT** — 20 for God bought you with a high price. So you must honor God with your body.
>
> **Luke 12:7 CSB** — 7 "Indeed, the hairs of your head are all counted. Don't be afraid; you are worth more than many sparrows."

Coins are found in the world's systems. Collectible coins can be found in circulation. How many times have you seen an orphaned coin on the sidewalk or in the street? Without perceived value the world takes no notice. However, the collector sees the potential value the world ignores, and when an immensely valuable one is located by the collector, it is immediately desired and taken out of the world's hands. It is hand-picked and chosen to be a part of the collection.

You can speak with the voice of Love.

Love Values Us

In the same way we were hand-picked and taken out of the world's system in order to be adopted into the Father's family. We've been translated from the kingdom of darkness into the kingdom of light! He greatly desired to adopt you into His beloved family!

> **Matthew 13:44-46 TLB** — 44 "The Kingdom of Heaven is like a treasure a man discovered in a field. In his excitement, he sold everything he owned to get enough money to buy the field—and get the treasure, too! 45 "Again, the Kingdom of Heaven is like a pearl merchant on the lookout for choice pearls. 46 He discovered a real bargain—a pearl of great value—and sold everything he owned to purchase it!
>
> **1 Peter 2:9 VOICE** — 9 But you are a chosen people, set aside to be a royal order of priests, a holy nation, God's own; so that you may proclaim the wondrous acts of the One who called you out of inky darkness into shimmering light.

Circulated coins are found abused, dirty, grimy, and sticky because of how the world treated them. The collector will set up a cleaning

Love is a healing salve to the soul and body.

station using non-harmful chemicals and water. The collector will take each coin, gently clean it, and air dry it with a soft absorbent material. Like us, we came to the Lord with many issues wrong and He cleaned us up. He saw our hurts, He saw our faults, He saw our mistakes, He saw our abuse, He saw our struggles, and yet He saw value in us we ourselves could not see. He cleaned us up, healed our bodies, mended our hearts, restored our joy, removed our fears, delivered us from devils, and now we can be identified as His. We could not see who we were under the abuse of the world but now that we have been cleansed we can see who we always were.

> **1 Peter 2:10 NLT —** 10 "Once you had no identity as a people; now you are God's people. Once you received no mercy; now you have received God's mercy."
>
> **Galatians 4:4-7 ERV —** 4 But when the right time came, God sent His Son, who was born from a woman and lived under the law. 5 God did this so that He could buy the freedom of those who were under the law. God's purpose was to make

Love chose you.

us His children. 6 Since you are now God's children, He has sent the Spirit of His Son into your hearts. The Spirit cries out, " Abba, Father." 7 Now you are not slaves like before. You are God's children, and you will receive everything He promised His children.

Now, that the coins are dry and recognizable, they are ready for display. Depending on how the collector wants their coins to be seen, there are many methods to store coins. Arguably, the best method is called the, "slab," method. The coin is placed in a tamper-proof plastic case that allows the coin to be seen and protects it from all environmental hazards. Now that we've been cleaned up, we are placed into, "The Slab," Jesus Christ the Cornerstone, and hand-placed into the Father's family for all to see. He has His watchful eye on us making sure no one can harm or steal us away.

John 10:27-29 CSB — 27 "My sheep hear My voice, I know them, and they follow Me. 28 "I give them eternal life, and they will never perish. No one will snatch them out of My hand. 29 "My Father, who has given them to Me, is

You hear the whispers of Love in your life.

greater than all. No one is able to snatch them out of the Father's hand.

We are the coins that God Himself has collected from the far reaches of the Earth. He desired us to be a part of His family. He wanted to show us our true identity. He wanted to save us from the hurt of the world. He greatly desired to heal us, restore us, and deliver us. He brought us into His own house to share with us His blessings. He has chosen us to live in Christ the Cornerstone to reflect His glory for all to see. Praise the Lord for His faithful and unconditional love! We are immeasurably valuable to God!

Love is so glad you chose Him.

live victoriously

CHAPTER 9
Never-ending Love

Love is eternal. How do we define eternal? Let us see what the Bible tells us.

> In Hebrew the word for eternal is, "olam [Strongs H5769]." It means, "that which is perpetual, everlasting."
>
> In Greek the word is, "aionios [Strongs G166]." And it translates to, "that which has no beginning and no end."

Love never ends, never stops, never exhausts itself, and never gives up. This quality of love is why people have trouble after losing a relationship. There was never supposed to be a divorce or separation. It is a foreign concept to a being made to live forever. Love is committed to take care of one another. Jesus even talked about divorce in Mark 10.

> **Mark 10:2 NLT** — 2 Some Pharisees came and tried to trap Him with this question: "Should a man be allowed to divorce his wife?"

The Pharisees were not trying to get a real answer here. They were trying to get Jesus to say

 Love never never never gives up on anyone.

something incriminating that would turn His followers against Him, and also get Him in trouble with the Sanhedrin council. Based on Jesus' answer, He might offend everyone who has divorced a wife. Women were not well-regarded in Jewish society. They had nearly no rights and relied heavily on a husband or father to provide for them.

Originally, a man could only divorce his wife if she was found to be doing something shameful sexually, exposing her nakedness to others, or doing something that brought shame upon the family, but the religious political groups of the day added their own, "interpretations," to circumvent the law. A man could divorce his wife for any reason at all. It could be something as innocuous as a dinner that turned out bad. All he had to do was write a bill of divorcement and that was that. She was ousted out of his house with nothing.

It must have been hard to be a wife in that time period. The commitment from a man was not there. They had to perform well all the time for one little mistake is it all it might take for them to lose everything. What a terrible life to live! This

Love endures at all times.

was not the intended sign that marriage was supposed to be to the world!

> **Mark 10:3 NLT —** 3 Jesus answered them with a question: "What did Moses say in the law about divorce?"

Jesus was wise. He turned the question back on them. He knew the law inside and out. He studied it judiciously. He wanted to see what they would say, so He could hear the intent of their heart.

> **Mark 10:4 NLT —** 4 "Well, he permitted it," they replied. "He said a man can give his wife a written notice of divorce and send her away."

They parroted back the law and blamed Moses for divorce. They refused to take responsibility for their incorrect application of the law. They tried to find any way they could to bypass the law.

> **Mark 10:5 NLT —** 5 But Jesus responded, "He wrote this commandment only as a concession to your hard hearts.

This is an amazing statement! Moses is the one that instituted divorce. It was never sanctioned by

Love hears every heart's cry.

God! Moses, in his earthly wisdom, decided that divorce was necessary. He made up the idea and wrote it into the law which the people followed (Maybe he thought it was better than them killing each other?). However, the divorcement was based on the woman's purity. It was supposed to be an option only if she was found doing something shameful. But even in that, God never intended for marriage to end. It is an eternal covenant.

Paul, in Ephesians 5, elucidates that marriage is a symbol of Jesus' love for His bride. It is Jesus' responsibility to take care of His bride. In the same way, the husband is to take care of His wife. Marriage brings glory to God when He is at the center of it.

> **Mark 10:6 NLT** — 6 But 'God made them male and female' from the beginning of creation.

Jesus is speaking about Adam and Eve here. Eve was created from Adam. I have heard different interpretations of what that means. I have heard it said that God took the womb out of Adam and made woman. I have heard it said that this references DNA. The X and Y chromosomes were separated when they used to be joined together. The point is they were one being before, so they could not be separated.

> **Mark 10:7-8 NLT —** 7 'This explains why a man leaves his father and mother and is joined to his wife, 8 and the two are united into one.' Since they are no longer two but one,

Jesus is quoting Adam in verse 7 here. He is building on the previous verse saying that because male and female are two separate beings, but used to be one, they still retain their oneness. They are better together than apart. They cover for each other's weaknesses. They are the accepted model for God's family plan to populate the world with children. Because they have chosen to be together they are now one and operate as one being.

> **Mark 10:9 NLT —** 9 let no one split apart what God has joined together."

Jesus is saying that marriage joins people together. Man should not be tearing apart, manipulating, corrupting, or changing the natural

Righteousness is understood in the light of Love.

purpose of marriage by treating it like anything less than a full commitment that only death can break. God never ever has any second thoughts about us. He is fully committed to us in a marriage covenant. We are Jesus' bride and He will take care of us for all eternity!

When we accepted Jesus as Lord, He became our Husband. He will provide for His bride. He will make sure she is safe. He will make sure she is able to enjoy the best things in life. He will comfort her when she is down. He will satisfy her with love. He will be there for her when she is feeling alone or hurt. He never even thinks about running out on her. Jesus is the archetype for all husbands.

> **2 Corinthians 11:2 VOICE** — 2 To be completely honest, I am extremely jealous for you; but it's the same kind of jealousy God has for you. You see, like an attentive father, I have pledged your hand in marriage and promised to present you as a pure virgin to the One who would be your husband, the Anointed One.
>
> **Isaiah 54:5 ERV** — 5 Your real husband is the One who made you. His name is the Lord All-

Love is married to your heart.

Never-ending Love

Powerful. The Holy One of Israel is your Protector, and He is the God of all the earth!

Jesus joined Himself to us. We are inextricably joined together in one spirit with Him. We cannot ever be torn asunder!

> **1 Corinthians 6:17 NIV** — 17 But whoever is united with the Lord is one with Him in spirit.

God will never ever forsake us for any reason. We never have to doubt if God loves us. That is how good eternal never-ending Love is! He is committed to us forever!

Love could not be more committed to you.

CHAPTER ∞

The Love Chapter: 1 Cor. 13

Paul wrote a detailed explanation of Love in 1 Corinthians 13. It is one of the most famous chapters in the Bible. You hear it read at weddings, engagements, and anniversaries. It represents a beautiful picture of Love. We are going to dive into the meaning of each verse as it pertains to Love.

> **1 Corinthians 13:1 KJV —** 1 "Though I speak with the tongues of men and of angels, and have not charity, I am become as sounding brass, or a tinkling cymbal."

A clanging cymbal or noisy gong is not a nice sound. It would be annoying, unwanted, and a nuisance. It would drown out what you actually want to hear. It would drive people away. Nobody in their right mind would want to listen to it. This is how important love is.

When we try to serve God or others outside of love, it becomes an annoyance. "Look at me, I am a nice person. I donated clothes to the poor. I served homeless people at the soup kitchen. I picked up all the trash alongside the road near my house. Look how good I am!" People can tell when others are fake. They can see that they are

---

Love is writing each chapter of your life.

not doing this for the person; they are doing it for themselves. Jesus called out the Pharisees and Sadducees about this. They would parade around like they were better than anyone else.

> **Matthew 23:2-7 ERV —** 2 "The teachers of the law and the Pharisees have the authority to tell you what the Law of Moses says. 3 So you should obey them. Do everything they tell you to do. But their lives are not good examples for you to follow. They tell you to do things, but they don't do those things themselves. 4 They make strict rules that are hard for people to obey. They try to force others to obey all their rules. But they themselves will not try to follow any of those rules. 5 "The only reason they do what they do is for other people to see them. They make the little Scripture boxes they wear bigger and bigger. And they make the tassels on their prayer clothes long enough for people to notice them. 6 These men love to have the places of honor at banquets and the most important seats in the synagogues. 7 They love for people to show respect to them in the marketplaces and to call them 'Teacher.'

Nobody wanted to hear them spout on about

Love prefers others first.

their good deeds; it drove people away from the Lord. We are not like that though. When we speak to people: we speak out of love.

> **1 Corinthians 13:2 KJV —** 2 "And though I have the gift of prophecy, and understand all mysteries, and all knowledge; and though I have all faith, so that I could remove mountains, and have not charity, I am nothing."

This is amazing! Even someone who has all wisdom, knowledge, and faith to do miracles can operate without love! You can have faith to do good works but still not love others, not care about others, and not have compassion for others. It all avails to nothing if you use your gifts for personal gain or glory. Jesus told His disciples that there will be many that said they did things for Him but that He will tell them that He never knew them. They did it for themselves: even using the name of Jesus for gain. All because they did not do it from Love!

> **Matthew 7:21-23 ERV —** 21 "Not everyone who calls Me Lord will enter God's kingdom. The only people who will enter are those who do what my

God loves you more than you can comprehend.

Father in heaven wants. 22 On that last Day many will call Me Lord. They will say, 'Lord, Lord, by the power of Your name we spoke for God. And by Your name we forced out demons and did many miracles.' 23 Then I will tell those people clearly, 'Get away from Me, you people who do wrong. I never knew you.'

Wisdom does not guarantee you will love others. All the wisdom in the world does not amount to anything if it is not shared. To have wisdom for yourself and not to use it to benefit others is the epitome of selfishness. Solomon in all his great wisdom was led astray by many women. He knew they would lead him away. It was in the law that you should not intermarry with the women from pagan nations.

> **Deuteronomy 7:2-4 NLV** — 2 When the Lord your God gives them to you and you win the battles against them, you must destroy all of them. Make no agreement with them and show no favor to them. 3 Do not take any of them in marriage. Do not give your daughters to their sons. And do not take their daughters for your sons. 4 For they will turn your sons away from

Love is limitless.

following Me to serve other gods. Then the anger of the Lord will burn against you. And He will be quick to destroy you.

It was customary in Biblical times to have a treaty sealed by a marriage to a royal. Even in the name of peace, Solomon could not maintain his purity. He thought too high of himself and disobeyed the Lord and it destroyed him. What if he would have asked his advisors or the priests of the Law? Would they have been able to help him see the folly of marrying so many women in the name of, "peace?" We do not know but we trust that God is working wisdom in us through love.

> **1 Corinthians 13:3 KJV —** 3 "And though I bestow all my goods to feed the poor, and though I give my body to be burned, and have not charity, it profiteth me nothing."

People can sacrifice themselves to get glory. It is a sense of pride; it draws attention to oneself. To die for oneself is selfishness. Without love, sacrifice or martyrdom is worthless. Doing something because you are wanting to get glory out of it is not love. Jesus told us not to boast

Love accomplishes the impossible.

when we give and do not let our right hand know what our left hand is doing.

> **Matthew 6:1-4 ERV —** 1 "Be careful! When you do something good, don't do it in front of others so that they will see you. If you do that, you will have no reward from Your Father in heaven. 2 "When you give to those who are poor, don't announce that you are giving. Don't be like the hypocrites. When they are in the synagogues and on the streets, they blow trumpets before they give so that people will see them. They want everyone to praise them. The truth is, that's all the reward they will get. 3 So when you give to the poor, don't let anyone know what you are doing. 4 Your giving should be done in private. Your Father can see what is done in private, and He will reward you.

We do not blow trumpets and announce that we have done something selfless in this life. The Pharisees enjoyed puffing themselves up and making themselves seem holier-than-thou. Jesus strongly rebuked them for it. We should only boast in the love Jesus has for us all.

1 Corinthians 13:4 KJV — 4 "Charity suffereth

Through love, we can endure persecution.

long, and is kind; charity envieth not; charity vaunteth not itself, is not puffed up,"

We are now talking about the attributes of Love. Love endures through hard times with bravery. Love does not become jealous but understands the one who is the object of affection. It is like a parent unconditionally loving their child even if that child does not reciprocate the same feelings at this time. The parent will not stop loving that child for any reason. The child's response is not taken into consideration because the child is born from the parent; the parent will always care for that child regardless if the child shows affection or love. It is a picture of our God. Even before we knew Him, He loved us. There is nothing we can do that can make Him stop loving us. He has chosen us to love for all eternity.

Love is kind and gentle and seeks the benefit of the other party. It is never harsh or overbearing. God is a gentleman. He will not barge into your life if you do not want Him around. Love is humble and meek and does not seek acclaim.

God looks for those who will seek His love.

> **1 Corinthians 13:5 KJV —** 5 "Doth not behave itself unseemly, seeketh not her own, is not easily provoked, thinketh no evil;"

Love does not make a show of itself. Love does not interrupt or create drama. Love is not self-serving. it wants the best for you but will love regardless if you ever return the love.

Remember the parable of the prodigal son? That son was not behaving in a loving manner. He asked for his inheritance ahead of time. Which means, "Father, I wish you were dead. Give me the wealth that I would get when you die." The father does not bat an eye. He does it. He gives him all that he would have got in the will.

> **Luke 15:12 NLT —** 12 The younger son told his father, 'I want my share of your estate now before you die.' So his father agreed to divide his wealth between his sons.

The son leaves home, thinking he has got a better life ahead of him because he is not stuck at home with his family. He wastes all his money with riotous living.

Trust in Love and you will never fail.

The Love Chapter: 1 Cor. 13

> **Luke 15:13 NLT —** 13 "A few days later this younger son packed all his belongings and moved to a distant land, and there he wasted all his money in wild living.

He ends up becoming a pig feeder; the lowest of the low for a Jew. Pigs are unclean animals to the Jews who would have no part with them. He becomes so hungry that he wishes for the pigs' food! What a crazy turn of events!

> **Luke 15:14-16 NLT —** 14 About the time his money ran out, a great famine swept over the land, and he began to starve. 15 He persuaded a local farmer to hire him, and the man sent him into his fields to feed the pigs. 16 The young man became so hungry that even the pods he was feeding the pigs looked good to him. But no one gave him anything.

He remembers the good times at his father's farm. He convinces himself to go see him.

> **Luke 15:17 NLT —** 17 "When he finally came to his senses, he said to himself, 'At home even the hired servants have food enough to spare, and here I am dying of hunger!

Love produces joy everlasting.

He feels he lost his sonship by disrespecting his father and hurting his brother, but he did not lose his sonship. You cannot lose that relationship. It is a part of your identity. We cannot lose our sonship in God because it is who we are now. Love does not remember when it is wronged. A child cannot change who their parents are. Their parents will always be their parents. Our Father will always be our Father no matter what we do.

> **Luke 15:18-19 NLT —** 18 I will go home to my father and say, "Father, I have sinned against both heaven and you, 19 and I am no longer worthy of being called your son. Please take me on as a hired servant."'

When the son gets near his home, the father runs out ahead. The father was looking for his son. He never gave up on him. He ran to him, and embraced him.

> **Luke 15:20 NLT —** 20 "So he returned home to his father. And while he was still a long way off, his father saw him coming. Filled with love and compassion, he ran to his son, embraced him, and kissed him.

Love raises orphans into sons and daughters.

The Love Chapter: 1 Cor. 13

The son apologized and asked to be made like the servants to work for his food and living. But the father completely ignores his requests. He calls him son. He gives him a royal signet ring representing authority. He gives him a robe representing forgiveness and coverage of sin. And he gives him sandals to walk in peace. Then the father slays the fatted calf and throws a huge party inviting all the neighbors around to celebrate his son coming home. What a picture of Love!

The father could have been harsh. He could have made his son work for his living. He could have blamed the son for making bad decisions. He did none of the above. It was as if he never acknowledged that the son did anything wrong. Almost like it was blotted out or completely eradicated from memory. Our sins were wiped away for good. God never brings them up to us. He will only reveal sin in our lives because He wants us to live in health, blessing, and prosperity. Sin can prevent us from reaching our potential.

> **Luke 15:21-24 NLT** — 21 His son said to him, 'Father, I have sinned against both heaven and

Love produces righteous living.

you, and I am no longer worthy of being called your son.' 22 "But his father said to the servants, 'Quick! Bring the finest robe in the house and put it on him. Get a ring for his finger and sandals for his feet. 23 And kill the calf we have been fattening. We must celebrate with a feast, 24 for this son of mine was dead and has now returned to life. He was lost, but now he is found.' So the party began.

Love forgets when it was last hurt. It does not hold grudges. The older brother of the prodigal took issue with the his younger brother coming back without punishment. He wanted to see justice done. He wanted him to have to work hard to get his sonship back, but love does not hold things against another. Love takes no offense unlike the brother who became so offended the father had to convince him to come to the party. Love does not turn to bitterness if it is rejected. The father had every right to be bitter about what his son did to Him. Yet He gave it no thought.

Luke 15:28-32 NLT — 28 "The older brother was angry and wouldn't go in. His father came out

Love does not condemn.

and begged him, 29 but he replied, 'All these years I've slaved for you and never once refused to do a single thing you told me to. And in all that time you never gave me even one young goat for a feast with my friends. 30 Yet when this son of yours comes back after squandering your money on prostitutes, you celebrate by killing the fattened calf!' 31 "His father said to him, 'Look, dear son, you have always stayed by me, and everything I have is yours. 32 We had to celebrate this happy day. For your brother was dead and has come back to life! He was lost, but now he is found!'"

Love does not insult, make coarse jokes, or snipe others. It is gentle, caring, and speaks only good of the other party. Praise the Lord for His wondrous love!

1 Corinthians 13:6 KJV — 6 "Rejoiceth not in iniquity, but rejoiceth in the truth;"

Love reveals truth. Unrighteousness or the law is not what Love wants. Love wants to reveal truth: not pronounce judgment. Love desires for truth to be made known to all. John 8:32 says it is

Love creates the best possible blessings for your life.

the truth you know that will set you free.

> **John 8:32 NKJV** — 32 "And you shall know the truth, and the truth shall make you free."

The truth is we have been set free from the bondage of sin, the law, and death because of the death, burial, and resurrection of Jesus. We believe on Him and have been made free!

> **1 Corinthians 13:7 KJV** — 7 "Beareth all things, believeth all things, hopeth all things, endureth all things."

Love does not quit. There is no condition that can make Love give up. Love will continually try to reach you. Love cannot deny itself. Love does not compromise but perseveres with faith and hope while enduring all manner of attacks. Similar to how a barricade or Roman Garrison marches down enemy lines while protecting each other. Love cannot be taken down by the enemy. Love fights for every heart: always hopeful that it will reach each person.

> **1 Corinthians 13:8 KJV** — 8 "Charity never faileth: but whether there be prophecies, they shall fail;

God is loving you into all truth and knowledge.

The Love Chapter: 1 Cor. 13

whether there be tongues, they shall cease; whether there be knowledge, it shall vanish away."

Nothing is as important as Love. Other things eventually lose their effectiveness but Love does not. Love does not go out of season. Love is known throughout history. Acts of love are remembered forever.

> **1 Corinthians 13:9-10 KJV** — 9 "For we know in part, and we prophesy in part. 10 But when that which is perfect is come, then that which is in part shall be done away."

We only see a part of the full picture. We cannot truly understand Love in this life. It goes beyond what our minds are capable of processing. What little we know of Love we know that we want it and desire it deeply. Love is infinite. There is always another aspect to learn. When we get to Heaven, then we can truly experience Love in His full glory.

> **1 Corinthians 13:11-12 KJV** — 11 "When I was a child, I spake as a child, I understood as a child, I thought as a child: but when I became a man,

Love raises the standard of favor for you.

I put away childish things. 12 For now we see through a glass, darkly; but then face to face: now I know in part; but then shall I know even as also I am known."

Children play with their own things. After they reach adulthood they give up childish things. Like the distortion of a funhouse mirror or like one triangle that is a part of a kaleidoscopic pattern. When we know the full picture of Love... we will not remember the old way. The way we perceive Love now is incomplete compared to the way we will when He is fully revealed to us. It is like looking at a puzzle that is missing many of the pieces. You can make out some of the detail but not all of it. After we learn about Love we are able to fill in more of the puzzle. We now know Love so we do not dwell on the past things we were taught like the law or traditions of men that attempt to earn righteousness. We know better that through Christ we have been made righteous.

1 Corinthians 13:13 KJV — 13 "And now abideth faith, hope, charity, these three; but the

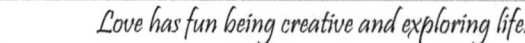
Love has fun being creative and exploring life.

greatest of these is charity."

Faith in God is rewarded in the next life so it will last. Hope is an expectation of good which can be carried until the end of our life where it is fulfilled in God. Love drew us near and took care of us until the end so, we will always experience Love forever. Love causes us to believe in faith and hope for a better tomorrow.

Wow! We covered a copious amount of material here. God is so good to us. His love is what sets Him and us apart from the world. We can love in difficult situations. We can love when we are openly being mocked or persecuted. We can love when we do not, "feel," like it in the flesh. We can choose to love anyone at anytime. We can be a living Love chapter for Jesus to reach out to all!

you are loved by Me.

We can love because Love defines our personality.

CHAPTER 8
Taste and See Love

God wants us to taste and see how much He loves us. Everyone needs the love only He can give. I was studying Acts one day and saw a spiritual interaction between Saul and Stephen. I believe this is what Holy Spirit was revealing to me. Saul had never experienced the love of God.

Saul was a religious zealot. He was deeply committed to Moses' law. He was the penultimate Pharisee. He was brought up to follow every command of the law. He knew only the rote rules. He had taken an oath to be obedient to them all. The laws were strict and did not allow any interpretation.

Saul's entire life was spent doing and working out his own righteousness. Then comes along, "The Way." A radical movement that was turning people away from the law of Moses. The people dedicated to this movement were willing to die for this supposed resurrected Man, "Jesus Christ." What is a passionate Pharisee to do? In his mind, the world is going the wrong way and he had the power to do something about it.

He hears about a man doing all sorts of miracles in the name of a man named, "Jesus Christ." This, "Stephen," knows His history. He

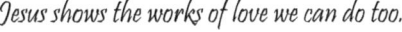

Jesus shows the works of love we can do too.

presents a long dissertation trying to convince others to follow this, "Jesus Christ," who he is calling, "The Messiah." Saul hears every word spoken by him. He thinks to himself, "How could this evil man have such fervent faith? How could he be so prideful in saying that the law of Moses is not needed anymore?" Saul began to wonder about these things. Stephen incites the crowd and Saul consents to his stoning. "This guy will be better off dead. Then he cannot pollute the chosen people of Israel with his false belief."

> **Acts 7:58-59 KJV —** 58 And cast him out of the city, and stoned him: and the witnesses laid down their clothes at a young man's feet, whose name was Saul. 59 And they stoned Stephen, calling upon God, and saying, Lord Jesus, receive my spirit.

He sees Stephen look up into the sky with a smile on his face. He cries out "Lord, lay not this sin to their charge." Saul thinks, "Even 'til death this man would not stop following this, 'Jesus Christ.'"

> **Acts 7:60 KJV —** 60 And he kneeled down, and

Love knows your name and every detail about you.

cried with a loud voice, Lord, lay not this sin to their charge. And when he had said this, he fell asleep.

Saul is not sure what to think. He had never seen such passionate faith in his life. Saul had some doubts but his Pharisaical beliefs were strongly ingrained in him.

Acts 8:3 KJV — 3 As for Saul, he made havock of the church, entering into every house, and haling men and women committed them to prison.

"There must be something more I can do!" Saul goes to the head priest and asks for papers to assert his authority to arrest these heretics and drag them to Jerusalem bound.

Acts 9:1-2 KJV — 1 And Saul, yet breathing out threatenings and slaughter against the disciples of the Lord, went unto the high priest, 2 And desired of him letters to Damascus to the synagogues, that if he found any of this way, whether they were men or women, he might bring them bound unto Jerusalem.

God is pleased with you because you trust Jesus.

Taste and See Love

All while this is happening, "The Way," is expanding and growing out of control. Saul begins to wonder about the things Stephen had said. Saul knew the history of his people. He could look into the scrolls and see what he was talking about. Saul was studious. He certainly had the time to examine and research everything Stephen said. All of Stephen's arguments were sound. Saul firmly believed he was doing God's will. Saul could see these scriptures and see Jesus in them but could not commit himself to it. He pondered this all throughout his journey to Damascus.

Saul is walking with others on the road to Damascus. He kept all these things in his heart. He wanted to know the truth. He was seeking it out as best as he could. Then all of a sudden, the brightest light he had ever witnessed shines all around him.

> **Acts 9:3 KJV** — 3 And as he journeyed, he came near Damascus: and suddenly there shined round about him a light from heaven:

"What is going on?!" Saul is panicking to himself. However, in himself he knows who this is.

Love makes miracles happen.

Taste and See Love

He saw Him in the scrolls. He saw His disciples perform miracles and healings in His name. It was undeniable that the one he had been persecuting is now here to judge him for missing it.

Saul feels a heavy glorious presence so much so that he cannot even stand. "This is unbelievable. The One I've been pursuing harshly is now ready to take me out. I should have accepted Him when I saw Him in the scrolls. Oh well. It is too late for me now." Then he hears the voice of Love. "Saul, Saul, why persecutest thou Me?"

> **Acts 9:4 KJV** — 4 And he fell to the earth, and heard a voice saying unto him, Saul, Saul, why persecutest thou Me?

Saul had never heard a voice so comforting, so peaceful, so... full of love! "How could I make the mistake to persecute this man. He surely is the Son of God." Saul just had to know for sure. He asked Jesus, "Who art thou, Lord?" Jesus answered, "I AM Jesus whom thou persecutest: it is hard for thee to kick against the pricks."

> **Acts 9:5 KJV** — 5 And he said, Who art thou,

Persecution and trials cannot snuff out Love.

Lord? And the Lord said, I AM Jesus whom thou persecutest: it is hard for thee to kick against the pricks.

"I have never felt a voice and presence so loving before. He truly is who I thought He was. I made a huge mistake but I do not feel any judgment coming from Him. Is this truly the God I have been following? I was taught God was a vengeful and judgmental God who barely tolerated our presence because of His great holiness and hate for sin. But this Jesus, He is not like that at all. I need to know more about Him. Maybe I can do something to offset my sin against Him." He asks Jesus, "Lord, what wilt thou have me to do?" Saul thinks, "Surely there must be something I can do to earn my righteousness. The law has taught me that we can only remove sin by blood. Maybe He'll have me do a sacrifice at the nearest synagogue? I hope He can forgive me." Jesus answered, "Arise, and go into the city, and it shall be told thee what thou must do."

Acts 9:6 KJV — 6 And he trembling and astonished said, Lord, what wilt thou have me

Love floods dark atmospheres with light.

Taste and See Love

to do? And the Lord said unto him, Arise, and go into the city, and it shall be told thee what thou must do.

Saul is thinking to himself, "Yes, Lord. He will direct me to the next step. I wonder what kind of sacrifice I will have to offer to get clean again? I wonder what ceremonies He will have me go through? I do remember some of His disciples were fishermen and tax collectors. How could they have enough knowledge or repent enough for their thievery to be a disciple of the Son of God? I just do not know. But I do know, He has put off judging me at this time. I will work my entire life to become worthy of His forgiveness."

At the same time, the voice of Jesus is heard by the other travelers. They are astonished at what they are hearing. Saul gets up and then realizes he cannot see. "This must be the judgment. Because I was blinded by my foolish ambition, He has blinded me as a way for me to atone for my sins." He accepts it and asks the men to take him to Damascus.

Acts 9:8 KJV — 8 And Saul arose from the earth;

 Love draws us with grace, kindness, and goodness.

and when his eyes were opened, he saw no man: but they led him by the hand, and brought him into Damascus.

For three days, He was blind and lived in darkness, but I really believe this was Jesus teaching him and showing him things to come. He lived in the light of the truth. He could have been caught up in visions and Heaven during this time. He fasted so he could get a stronger revelation of Jesus. Jesus was sustaining Him.

Acts 9:9 KJV — 9 And he was three days without sight, and neither did eat nor drink.

Three days he was practically dead in his body then he was resurrected by the power of Holy Spirit. Ready to do anything through Jesus who had mercy on him even though he killed many disciples. He was passionate and devoted to the loving Savior Jesus Christ.

The doubts about his own faith is what led to his Damascus road experience. Jesus saw the potential in Saul. He saw that he was truly seeking God. His heart was in the right place. He loved to bring God glory and to do what he was taught.

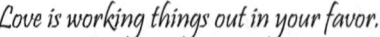

Love is working things out in your favor.

Taste and See Love

He believed the law was the only way to God. When Jesus appeared to him, I believe Saul's doubts were erased. He knew exactly who was there, but he had not had a revelation of Love. He was taught about the vengeful and jealous God.

He thought he was about to be judged. However, to his amazement, Jesus was accepting and loving: much unlike what he had thought. His name was changed from Saul to Paul as a way to remind himself that He was a different person. He realized Jesus was the Son of God and was determined to seek Him out no matter the cost. And he did, with fervent desire that shows forth in his writings. He wrote 2/3 of the New Testament and we can still learn so much from examining Paul's life.

> **Psalm 34:8 KJV** — 8 O taste and see that the LORD is good: blessed is the man that trusteth in Him.

We have the revelation of God's love. It encompasses all scripture. We can taste as much as we want. We can see it as far as we want to. There is no limit. As we seek God with all our

Understanding Love makes it easy to live in peace.

Taste and See Love

heart, He draws closer to us. Accept the love of God in your life, seek Him in all you do, trust in Him for all your needs, and you shall experience God in a way that will make all else pale in comparison!

As we seek Love, He will draw closer to us.

your heart and body.

CHAPTER 5
Love Walk

A great example of how Holy Spirit leads us in love was when I took part in a blind trust walk. I had not met my partner beforehand. We both did not know what to expect. I had decided I would be the one blindfolded at first. Halfway through we would switch positions. If you have not done a blind trust walk before I highly recommend it. We were in a park-like place with a trail through the woods. I had some trouble putting my blindfold on. By the grace of God it did not fall off!

    A blind trust walk is when you are blindfolded and you have a partner who has to lead you through a path with only the sense of touch. Speaking is disallowed. You and your partner will come up with a communication system based on touch. It is a novel concept. With your vision obscured your other senses become more activated. You hear and smell things more strongly. It was a wonderful experience.

    At the start of the trail, me and my partner are lined up. We have to both be silent. The trail started off easy. We walked straight for a while into the woods. My partner gently placed his hands on my back and around the shoulders to

Love has gone before you to make your paths safe.

indicate we are to move forward. If he hesitated his grip I knew I needed to stop. If it was a wide-open area he would take my arm and we would walk side-by-side. If it was a difficult area, with steps, trees, or turns, he would let go entirely to reposition himself to give more directed signals. He would gently pull on my shoes and direct which leg to step with. He would take my hands and put them on a guardrail or on the tree so I would know what is around me.

> **2 Corinthians 5:7 KJV —** 7 (For we walk by faith, not by sight:)

We are in the process of learning how He communicates with us. The language of Love. He is always giving us signals. We must pay attention. When things become difficult… He gives us more direction! He knows the path better than we do.

At first, I was hesitant to trust. My body tensed up and I was slow-moving. He was giving me signals but I did not know what they meant. Even though He knew He was leading me safely; I had to trust and take the steps. As I learned how he communicated, I felt more at rest. I did not tense

God enjoys journeying with us.

Love Walk

up as much. I was able to enjoy the journey instead of wonder what was next.

> **Matthew 11:29-30 ERV** — 29 Accept My teaching. Learn from Me. I am gentle and humble in spirit. And you will be able to get some rest. 30 Yes, the teaching that I ask you to accept is easy. The load I give you to carry is light."

A yoke directs the neck. When you control the neck you control the direction. As we take on Jesus' yoke, we are directed in love, rest, and peace. As we learn how Holy Spirit communicates with us, we will learn to rest in Him. He has our best interests at heart. He only has good things in store for us. Our safety is His utmost priority. He wants us to rest in His love as we walk through life together.

When we arrived to the halfway point, my partner and I switched. Now I was the one directing him. I had to communicate as best as I could to protect him from the dangers of the trail. I had a desire to protect him because he could not see where he was going. He was trusting me to lead him in safety. I would dare not break that

Every day gets better with Love.

child-like innocent trust. How much more does God our Father want to protect us!?

> **Luke 18:16-17 TLB** — 16-17 Then Jesus called the children over to Him and said to the disciples, "Let the little children come to Me! Never send them away! For the Kingdom of God belongs to men who have hearts as trusting as these little children's. And anyone who doesn't have their kind of faith will never get within the Kingdom's gates."

I took my time making sure my intentional instructions would make sense. If he did not understand the first time I would try another way. I made sure to keep trying until he understood what I was doing. I opened doors and moved obstacles to make the path easier. There was a difficult part where they had to walk over a steep rock then walk unto a low wooden balance-beam. I prepared in my head what I would do before I got there. It is much like our God who has prepared the path of least resistance ahead of time. He comforts and supports us as we journey through life with Him. If at first we do not understand... He continually tries other methods

Love keeps communicating until He gets through.

to get our attention. He does not give up on us! He wants to make sure we feel safe in His love as we travel through life.

My partner got through it as I held his hands to keep him balanced. As we got to the end of the journey and he took off the blindfold; he noticed we were in a completely different area than when we started. God takes us so far in our journey. When we finally open our eyes to look around, we are amazed at where we have traveled from and where we are!

> **Proverbs 3:5-6 VOICE —** 5 Place your trust in the Eternal; rely on Him completely; never depend upon your own ideas and inventions. 6 Give Him the credit for everything you accomplish, and He will smooth out and straighten the road that lies ahead.

The process of the trust walk is an allegory to how Holy Spirit leads us in Love. We are learning the language of Love. God has a unique and distinct way of communicating with you. As you learn to trust Him more you will experience more of Him. You will pick-up on His nudges. The way He speaks and leads you will not be a mystery. He

Love keeps us balanced and in our right mind.

will lead you into all peace. Rest will be easy for you. His goodness becomes easy to trust. You will wonder why you were trusting your eyes at all!

Faith is how God wants us to experience all the benefits that grace has provided. Once you get to that place, where you trust God more than yourself, your life will take on a new peace, a new rest, and a new meaning! Worries will be so far out of your mind and troubles will not bother you anymore. Your trust in God's Word will lead you into victory through any and all circumstances.

> **2 Corinthians 2:14 NKJV** — 14 Now thanks be to God who always leads us in triumph in Christ, and through us diffuses the fragrance of His knowledge in every place.

When you learn to decipher the language of Love, you will be secure, at peace, joyful, and thankful to Him. Life will be full of adventure! You will enjoy every moment of the journey as you walk it out with Love guiding you!

Love leads you to more favor and blessings.

CHAPTER 5

Partner with Love

I have been turned off by the phrase, "used of/by God." When I think of something being used it normally means one-time or only temporarily. We need to be careful with our words. Partnership I believe is a stronger relationship that we have with Christ. Being used sounds like a servant who has no veto power. However, we are children of God.

> **1 John 4:4 NKJV —** 4 You are of God, little children, and have overcome them, because He who is in you is greater than he who is in the world.

> **Revelation 21:7 VOICE —** 7 To the victors will go this inheritance: I will be their God, and they will be My children.

Would you use your child or would you rather partner with them? I believe God is saying that He wants to partner with us to bring the Kingdom of Heaven into every situation: not, "use," us or utilize us like tools. He treats us like family.

> **1 Corinthians 1:9 NLT —** 9 God will do this, for He is faithful to do what He says, and He has invited you into partnership with His Son, Jesus Christ our Lord.

God desires to partner with you to bring blessings.

He loves and cares for each of us in His own way which is the way we need to be loved. He knows that we want to see His Word come to pass in our lives. Once we make ourselves available, then He can partner with us. He is a gentleman and will not force His will on us.

Manipulative people use people. There is a much stronger relationship with partnership. It requires us to know Him. We must believe that when we understand His purpose for us and those around us that it will bring such freedom and clarity.

Partnership requires us to understand the benefits of partnering. It requires a, "Yes," on both sides. We have an, eternal, "Yes," in Jesus, and now He is waiting for us to say, "Yes," to Him. God cannot work through us without our consent.

> **2 Corinthians 1:20 NLT —** 20 For all of God's promises have been fulfilled in Christ with a resounding "Yes!" And through Christ, our "Amen" (which means "Yes") ascends to God for His glory.

Partnership depends on trust. You must trust

God has approved you to love others.

Partner with Love

the character of the person you are partnering with. You have to research and watch how they operate. It takes time to gather all the facts. We have the Bible, the written Word of God, to teach us all about His ways.

> **2 Timothy 3:16-17 TLB** — 16 The whole Bible was given to us by inspiration from God and is useful to teach us what is true and to make us realize what is wrong in our lives; it straightens us out and helps us do what is right. 17 It is God's way of making us well prepared at every point, fully equipped to do good to everyone.

We have the Living Word of God, Jesus, to talk with everyday.

> **1 John 4:15 TLB** — 15 Anyone who believes and says that Jesus is the Son of God has God living in him, and he is living with God.

We have Holy Spirit to bring revelation to us through the Word.

> **1 John 2:20 NLV** — 20 The Holy Spirit has been given to you and you all know the truth.

We have our Heavenly Father who provides us

You will bless others by your loving.

with everything we need.

> **Philippians 4:19 ERV** — 19 My God will use His glorious riches to give you everything you need. He will do this through Christ Jesus.

We have all the information we need to make an informed decision. We should partner with God in every area of our lives. It is a mutually beneficial covenant for both parties. God needs us to operate in the world and we need Him because only through Jesus can we be saved. It is a win-win!

I can hear some of you saying, "But God used prophets in the Old Testament. The Bible clearly states as such." God had to use prophets of old because He was not able to dwell in them. He had no other option but to clothe them temporarily in a fleeting moment.

> **Judges 6:34 NLT** — 34 Then the Spirit of the LORD took possession of Gideon. He blew a ram's horn as a call to arms, and the men of the clan of Abiezer came to him.

> **Judges 14:6 TLB** — 6 At that moment the Spirit of the Lord came mightily upon him and since

Love helps us make good decisions.

Partner with Love

he had no weapon, he ripped the lion's jaws apart and did it as easily as though it were a young goat! But he didn't tell his father or mother about it.

Ezekiel 11:5 TLB — 5 Then the Spirit of the Lord came upon me and told me to say: "The Lord says to the people of Israel: Is that what you are saying? Yes, I know it is, for I know everything you think—every thought that comes into your minds.

That is the definition of, "use." He could not partner with them because they were not holy. The holy cannot partner with the unholy, but now, in Christ, we have the same power that Jesus has.

Romans 8:11 NLT — 11 The Spirit of God, who raised Jesus from the dead, lives in you. And just as God raised Christ Jesus from the dead, He will give life to your mortal bodies by this same Spirit living within you.

The entirety of the Godhead exists in us. It is now possible for God to partner with us! He wants to partner with us! We have a choice in the matter. Do not be, "used," for a brief moment by

Love exists in you to bless your being.

God, but instead build a lasting partnership with Him to bring Heaven to Earth through the power of Holy Spirit operating in your life.

> **John 7:38 NKJV —** 38 "He who believes in Me, as the Scripture has said, out of his heart will flow rivers of living water."
>
> **Hebrews 13:20-21 VOICE —** 20 Now may the God of peace, who brought the great Shepherd of the sheep, our Lord Jesus, back from the dead through the blood of the new everlasting covenant, 21 perfect you in every good work as you work God's will. May God do in you only those things that are pleasing in His sight through Jesus the Anointed, our Liberating King, to whom we give glory always and forever. Amen.

Jesus watches over His sheep with loving tender care.

goodness toward you.

CHAPTER 5

Love Cleanses Lepers

Have you ever thought, why did Jesus single lepers out? Was it because this represents people ostracized in society? Surely leprosy is considered a sickness so we cannot consider it a redundancy; Jesus always spoke with intention and purpose.

> **Matthew 10:8 NKJV —** 8 "Heal the sick, cleanse the lepers, raise the dead, cast out demons. Freely you have received, freely give."

I believe this is referring to freedom. Lepers were completely ignored by society: cast off into their own village away from the public. It was an arduous process to get out of this life. There were many rules and regulations that had to be passed before you were free to leave. Lepers were bound to the stigma surrounding their diseases.

I believe that cleansing refers to setting them free from bondage. They would be free to walk around in public and associate with others. Their identity is no longer defined by their disease. They are a new being in Christ. They are free from the condemnation that followed them all their life. Cleansing the lepers refers to resetting the identity of someone who is lost in guilt, shame, bondage to life choices, addictions,

---

 God demonstrates that our true identity is Love.

condemnation, and sin. This could be understood scripturally as, "mending of broken hearts." Jesus accepted them, and they found healing and wholeness in Him for their hearts and bodies.

> **John 8:36 VOICE** — 36 So think of it this way: if the Son comes to make you free, you will really be free.

> **2 Corinthians 5:17 TLB** — 17 When someone becomes a Christian, he becomes a brand new person inside. He is not the same anymore. A new life has begun!

We are to show people their identity in Christ and pull them out of their, "leprosy." The self-condemnation that eats away at their very heart. They will find restoration in Jesus and be able to enjoy life and not feel alone and unwanted.

> **Romans 8:1 KJV** — 1 There is therefore now no condemnation to them which are in Christ Jesus, who walk not after the flesh, but after the Spirit.

> **Luke 4:18 TLB** — 18 "The Spirit of the Lord is upon me; He has appointed me to preach Good News to the poor; He has sent me to heal the

Love breaks chains, delivers, and sets free.

Love Cleanses Lepers

brokenhearted and to announce that captives shall be released and the blind shall see, that the downtrodden shall be freed from their oppressors, and that God is ready to give blessings to all who come to Him."

There are many people who need deliverance. They do not know that in Jesus they can find their freedom from all bondages. We must be willing to show, "lepers," they are beloved of God. We can teach them their true identity in Christ. Through Love we can cleanse the, "lepers," of society and show them Who really defines them.

Grace from favoring you

Holy Spirit empowers us with Love.

CHAPTER 3

Sowing and Reaping in Love

If you give in love you will reap in love. Giving to God out of a cheerful or thankful heart is giving in love. You know that God will use the finances you give Him to love others. He will, in turn, send love gifts your way. Giving to God can also be donating your time to helping others. Whatever you give, you will receive back of the same type multiplied by God's favor. God is abundant and generous. He enjoys blessing His kids.

> **2 Corinthians 9:7-8 NKJV** — 7 So let each one give as he purposes in his heart, not grudgingly or of necessity; for God loves a cheerful giver. 8 And God is able to make all grace abound toward you, that you, always having all sufficiency in all things, may have an abundance for every good work.
>
> **Isaiah 43:19 VOICE** — 19 Watch closely: I am preparing something new; it's happening now, even as I speak, and you're about to see it. I am preparing a way through the desert; Waters will flow where there had been none.

Since 2009, I wanted a blue acoustic-electric guitar. I kept telling myself one day I would buy a good one. I said I would buy one once I got my

Love looks for every opportunity to bless you.

MCITP (Microsoft Certified Information Technology Professional) certification. That never happened as I went in a different direction with my career. Anytime I thought about it; I could not justify the expense in my budget. My friend, Joseph, said something to the effect of, "God will get you a new guitar so be expecting." I said, "Sure He can," but in my heart, I was not convinced He would. A couple years later, I had forgotten the whole encounter. The thought never crossed my mind.

It was the day of my birthday in 2020. We had guest speakers, Ashley and Carlie Terradez visiting our church. One of their topics was about sowing and instantly reaping. I felt the passion of God to give. I asked the Lord, "How much should I give?" He asked, "How much would you be willing to give?" I said my number, He gave me a number that was much higher. At first I hesitated, I had given more before but why was this bothering me? I decided that since God requested it, He has a reason for it. I gave the amount as indicated by God. Really tried not to think too hard about it. Money has a way of sticking in the mind. Satan

Love remembers your desires and dreams.

Sowing and Reaping in Love

always comes back with, "Did you really just give that much away for nothing?!" I shut him up by saying, "God is my Source, He will provide for me. Since God asked for it, He needed it more than me." I went home still thinking about it.

My brother and friends were waiting at the house. They had made plans for my birthday. I saw them briefly before heading to my room to dress down from church. I was still thinking about the money. I had settled in my heart that was the right amount yet there was a nagging doubt that I thought I had gotten over. I kept arguing with myself and saying God will provide for me. I left my room and met up with my brother and friends. They said they had some gifts for me. They gifted me some cool things. I am thankful to have such great friends and family!

Nick, one of mine and brother's closest friends said he had a surprise for me. I had no idea what it would be. He went to my brother's room and came out with a brand new blue acoustic-electric guitar... I was floored! It was everything I had wanted in a guitar. Nick, said as was walking through the music store, this guitar caught his

Love is always giving us more than enough.

eye. It was a beauty and it was not cheap either! Everyone wanted to help buy it but Nick waved them off. He said he wanted to buy it. After all the things I had blessed him with over the years; this was a small token of his gratitude.

I could not have been more surprised! God does not forget our wants. His timing is perfect. I was nearly in tears. I was overwhelmed with joy and thankfulness. As I was putting it away, I heard God say, "This guitar is because you have been faithful to give to Me." I thanked Him and firmly settled in my heart that anytime God wants me to give that I will without any wavering or doubt.

> **Proverbs 11:24 ERV** — 24 Some people give freely and gain more; others refuse to give and end up with less.

I gave in love and received in love. You can too! There are plenty of opportunities to give to God. Volunteering in church, donating time to a para-church ministry, giving of finances, and helping a neighbor or family member are a few ways you can give in love. Expect to receive from God when you give in love!

The provision of Love exceeds our every need.

Sowing and Reaping in Love

Another way we sow love is by working a job! Did you know working is loving? The CEO is like a parent taking care of children who work with them. They are receiving the blessing and sharing with everyone else. They direct the flow so as to make sure all needs are met.

The CEO cannot do it all by themself. They need trustworthy workers to partner with. Work is always for someone's benefit; whether it is to take care of your needs to bless others or the service provided is a direct blessing to another.

Working is good! We have been designed with an ability to get work done. We can appreciate a well-done job. Then when we rest from our labors we can reflect on the goodness of our God to provide for us and for others. God wants you to work! It is how He establishes the covenant of blessing with Abraham.

> **Deuteronomy 8:18 NKJV** — 18 "And you shall remember the LORD your God, for it is He who gives you power to get wealth, that He may establish His covenant which He swore to your fathers, as it is this day.
>
> **Ecclesiastes 2:24 NKJV** — 24 Nothing is better for

 Work is a blessing given to us by Love.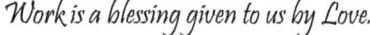

Sowing and Reaping in Love

a man than that he should eat and drink, and that his soul should enjoy good in his labor. This also, I saw, was from the hand of God.

Working is giving of your time and energy. Working is giving. There is a law of sowing and reaping in the Kingdom of God. Give God something to bless! We work so we can bless others and sometimes the work itself is the blessing. God is not mocked; He shall surely multiply whatever you give Him! You can never out give God. Praise the Lord for teaching us to sow in love through working!

> **Psalm 37:26 NLT** — 26 The godly always give generous loans to others, and their children are a blessing.
>
> **Proverbs 10:22 NKJV** — 22 The blessing of the LORD makes one rich, And He adds no sorrow with it.
>
> **Luke 6:38 VOICE** — 38 Don't hold back—give freely, and you'll have plenty poured back into your lap—a good measure, pressed down, shaken together, brimming over. You'll receive in the same measure you give.

Sow in Love and receive a great harvest.

Sowing and Reaping in Love

We can sow and reap in love by working; by giving of our time; by donating and gifting ministries and charities (doing the work of the Lord); by volunteering at church, by helping neighbors, family, and friends; and by ministering with your God-given gifts. I am sure you can come up with some ways to start sowing. Expect to reap a bountiful harvest because Love always gives back!

You were created to love like Me.

Trust that Love is tending your fields of blessing.

CHAPTER 4
Love Like Jesus

Compassion is a choice that no matter what happens, you cannot leave the other person in the condition they are; you are forced into action by your heart. You have a fervent desire to do whatever you can to help them. How much the Father must have felt this way after man sinned! He did everything He possibly could to pull man out of their fallen state. Sending Jesus was the culmination of eternal compassion on mankind.

The Father was not content just rescuing a few. He wants to save all. Jesus could do something about man. Every decision God made had this forethought. He worked everything out to get Jesus to Earth as quickly as possible. That is a real unconditional love.

We all have this capacity for compassion. I can remember when I was visiting in-home hospice for Chaplaincy. One of my residents started having breathing trouble. Their husband also tweaked their knee while I was there. I could not leave them until I was assured they would be fine. He was her only caretaker. If something happened to him she would not get the care she needs. This ended up being late into the night. I helped both of them out. I imagine Jesus feeling

 Love cannot ignore suffering.

the same way about us. Scripture says He saw His people like sheep without a shepherd.

> **Matthew 9:36 NKJV** — 36 But when He saw the multitudes, He was moved with compassion for them, because they were weary and scattered, like sheep having no shepherd.

He could not abandon them! In that same fashion, I could not leave either. I had to see this through. I had to have firm confidence that they would be okay. I prayed with them. I assisted them. I did what I could to support them.

Jesus does the same with us. He is our Mediator. He prays for us and supports us with His peace and joy.

> **Job 9:33-34 ERV** — 33 I wish there were someone who could listen to both sides, someone to judge both of us in a fair way. 34 I wish someone could take away the threat of God's punishment. Then He would not frighten me anymore.

> **1 Timothy 2:5 NKJV** — 5 For there is one God and one Mediator between God and men, the Man Christ Jesus,

He will never leave or forsake us. He will do

Jesus intercedes in Love for us.

whatever He can to make sure we are okay. In fact, He already did by reclaiming what humankind had lost. We can trust and rest in His love for us. He has given us all the tools to live a successful and victorious life.

Being afraid to hurt others in love is an oxymoron. If you respond out of love then even if it hurts for a bit, like a band-aid ripping off, in the long run, it will heal. There may be initial rejection but the seed is planted. Love does not cause lasting damage. Love does not scar. Love is what people need even when they are not sure about it. We have the love of the Lord; it is a character trait of Jesus and included in the fruit of the Spirit.

> **Galatians 5:22-23 VOICE** — 22 The Holy Spirit produces a different kind of fruit: unconditional love, joy, peace, patience, kindheartedness, goodness, faithfulness, 23 gentleness, and self-control. You won't find any law opposed to fruit like this.

You have the fruit now! Acknowledge what you have and you will see it manifest. Look what Philemon says.

Love makes all the difference in the world.

> **Philemon 1:6-7 ERV** — 6 I pray that the faith you share will make you understand every blessing we have in Christ. 7 My brother, you have shown love to God's people, and your help has greatly encouraged them. What a great joy and encouragement that has been to me.

We are salt and light in the world. "Salt," for we prevent the world from falling into total corruption. "Light," because we show them the path through the darkness to Jesus.

> **Matthew 5:13-16 NLV** — 13 "You are the salt of the earth. If salt loses its taste, how can it be made to taste like salt again? It is no good. It is thrown away and people walk on it. 14 You are the light of the world. You cannot hide a city that is on a mountain. 15 Men do not light a lamp and put it under a basket. They put it on a table so it gives light to all in the house. 16 Let your light shine in front of men. Then they will see the good things you do and will honor your Father Who is in heaven.

We cannot be afraid to love. There will be people who will reject. Jesus said we would suffer persecution. There will be people who will say

---

Love has no worry or anxiety attached to it.

Love Like Jesus

nasty things and try to harm you, but He also commanded us to fear not because He conquered the world. Trust in Jesus is what it takes to love others.

> **John 15:20 NLT** — 20 Do you remember what I told you? 'A slave is not greater than the master.' Since they persecuted Me, naturally they will persecute you. And if they had listened to Me, they would listen to you.
>
> **John 16:33 NKJV** — 33 "These things I have spoken to you, that in Me you may have peace. In the world you will have tribulation; but be of good cheer, I have overcome the world."
>
> **1 John 5:4 VOICE** — 4 Everything that has been fathered by God overcomes the corrupt world. This is the victory that has conquered the world: our faith.

Obey Jesus because He is Love.

> **John 15:12 NLV** — 12 This is what I tell you to do: Love each other just as I have loved you.
>
> **1 John 4:16 NLT** — 16 We know how much God loves us, and we have put our trust in His love.

Love is bold and never shy.

God is Love, and all who live in Love live in God, and God lives in them.

Reach out to others in love! Look how bold Peter and John were when they came across the crippled man before entering synagogue. They knew what they carried. They believed the words Jesus said to them. They had compassion on this man. They could not leave him in the same state when they knew they had the power and authority to do something about his malady.

> **Acts 3:3-10 ERV —** 3 That day he saw Peter and John going into the Temple area. He asked them for money. 4 Peter and John looked at the crippled man and said, "Look at us!" 5 He looked at them; he thought they would give him some money. 6 But Peter said, "I don't have any silver or gold, but I do have something else I can give you. By the power of Jesus Christ from Nazareth—stand up and walk!" 7 Then Peter took the man's right hand and lifted him up. Immediately his feet and legs became strong. 8 He jumped up, stood on his feet, and began to walk. He went into the Temple area with them. He was walking and jumping and praising God. 9-10 All the people recognized him. They knew

Holy Spirit flows through Love.

he was the crippled man who always sat by the Beautiful Gate to beg for money. Now they saw this same man walking and praising God. They were amazed. They did not understand how this could happen.

Look at how many people this reached! All the people saw the man who was a crippled beggar from birth and gave God the glory! When we step out in faith to do what Jesus has commanded us, we will be reaching more than just that person. The light of Love will shine all around and draw attention to God.

Jesus healed all He came in contact with. Jesus had compassion on people and that is what allowed the gifts to flow.

> **Matthew 14:14 NKJV** — 14 And when Jesus went out He saw a great multitude; and He was moved with compassion for them, and healed their sick.
>
> **Galatians 5:6 TLB** — 6 And we to whom Christ has given eternal life don't need to worry about whether we have been circumcised or not, or whether we are obeying the Jewish ceremonies

Healing is an overflow of Love.

or not; for all we need is faith working through love.

If you cannot love your brothers and sisters then how can you love unbelievers who have yet to come to Jesus? When you see someone else suffering see them as your sibling. What would you do for your family to help them? Would you help them with finances, health, transportation, emotional needs? If you knew you had the cure to their ailments would you withhold it? The Bible says to withhold good is the same as doing bad.

> **Proverbs 3:27-29 NKJV** — 27 Do not withhold good from those to whom it is due, When it is in the power of your hand to do so. 28 Do not say to your neighbor, "Go, and come back, And tomorrow I will give it," When you have it with you. 29 Do not devise evil against your neighbor, For he dwells by you for safety's sake.

Look at the definition of the Hebrew word for "withhold."

> Withhold — mana [Strongs H4513]. - to withhold, hold back, keep back, refrain, deny, keep restrain, hinder

Love gives the very best it possibly can.

This is interesting. If you can help your neighbor now do not tell them later or put it off. Do it now! Faith is now! Healing is now! To not do good when it is in your power is to betray the trust of your neighbor. How is that love?

> **1 John 3:17 KJV** — 17 But whoso hath this world's good, and seeth his brother have need, and shutteth up his bowels of compassion from him, how dwelleth the love of God in him?
>
> **John 15:12-17 VOICE** — 12 My commandment to you is this: love others as I have loved you. 13 There is no greater way to love than to give your life for your friends. 14 You celebrate our friendship if you obey this command. 15 I don't call you servants any longer; servants don't know what the master is doing, but I have told you everything the Father has said to Me. I call you friends. 16 You did not choose Me. I chose you, and I orchestrated all of this so that you would be sent out and bear great and perpetual fruit. As you do this, anything you ask the Father in My name will be done. 17 This is My command to you: love one another.

Look at the definition for, "shutteth up."

God is always reaching out in Love to all.

> shut up — kleio [Strong's G2808] - To withhold compassion or to be devoid of pity for someone.
>
> To withhold rain from Heaven.
>
> To obstruct the entrance into the kingdom of Heaven.

This is an astounding statement! By not showing love to a believer in need we, "withhold rain from Heaven." Who is the rain from Heaven? That would be Jesus the Water of Life. You are missing out on blessing that person and so, it is akin to withholding rain.

Withholding rain was considered a curse in the Old Testament! The blessing comes from rain. Would you curse your brother by not helping them: letting evil have its way when you can do something about it? By not helping a person in need is to obstruct them from entering into the blessing of God or the Kingdom of Heaven. You might be hurting their faith and could prevent them from getting to where God wants them to be. You have become a hindrance to the love of God!

Love waters every dry area of the heart.

> **Galatians 5:7 TLB** — 7 You were getting along so well. Who has interfered with you to hold you back from following the truth?
>
> **Proverbs 14:21 NLT** — 21 It is a sin to belittle one's neighbor; blessed are those who help the poor.
>
> **1 John 3:14 VOICE** — 14 We know that we have crossed over from death to real life because we are devoted to true love for our brothers and sisters. Anyone who does not love lives among corpses.

The book of James talks about this very thing. We must show that we love people by our actions. Saying and not doing is the same as doing nothing. Look at the strong language James uses!

> **James 2:14-17 VOICE** — 14 Brothers and sisters, it doesn't make any sense to say you have faith and act in a way that denies that faith. Mere talk never gets you very far, and a commitment to Jesus only in words will not save you. 15 It would be like seeing a brother or sister without any clothes out in the cold and begging for food,

Love is proven by action.

and 16 saying, "Shalom, friend, you should get inside where it's warm and eat something," but doing nothing about his needs—leaving him cold and alone on the street. What good would your words alone do? 17 The same is true with faith. Without actions, faith is useless. By itself, it's as good as dead.

Love passionately and powerfully seeks the well-being of all humankind. That same power of love compelled Jesus to do great exploits to save us and destroy the works of Satan. In fact, Jesus was anointed for this purpose!

> **1 John 3:8 NKJV** — 8 He who sins is of the devil, for the devil has sinned from the beginning. For this purpose the Son of God was manifested, that He might destroy the works of the devil.
>
> **Acts 10:38 VOICE** — 38 You know God identified Jesus as the uniquely chosen One by pouring out the Holy Spirit on Him, by empowering Him. You know Jesus went through the land doing good for all and healing all who were suffering under the oppression of the evil one, for God was with Him.

Jesus had no issue reaching out to people

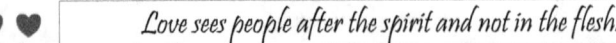
Love sees people after the spirit and not in the flesh.

who were trapped and oppressed by Satan. In fact, He wanted to restore all people. The same concept remains today. God wants unbelievers to be brought into His family. I believe that God can reach out to unbelievers. He can bless them, save their lives, rescue them, and watch over them. Sin is a distraction but God can still draw them in with His love. Grace is always stronger than sin.

> **Romans 5:20-21 TLB** — 20 The Ten Commandments were given so that all could see the extent of their failure to obey God's laws. But the more we see our sinfulness, the more we see God's abounding grace forgiving us. 21 Before, sin ruled over all men and brought them to death, but now God's kindness rules instead, giving us right standing with God and resulting in eternal life through Jesus Christ our Lord.

The world will recognize Jesus' disciples because of the love we show to each other and to them. I am sure God has no trouble showing love for the lost. Why should we? Dare to stand out. Be bold in Love! Go out of your way to bless someone else. The world needs Love and when they get ahold of Him, their lives are irrevocably

Love can bless whosoever He wants.

changed. Will God ever give up on anyone? No! Then we should not either!

> **Romans 2:4 TLB —** 4 Don't you realize how patient He is being with you? Or don't you care? Can't you see that He has been waiting all this time without punishing you, to give you time to turn from your sin? His kindness is meant to lead you to repentance.

In mathematics, there is a specific way to write multiplication of variables. When two variables or constants are side-by-side it means they are multiplied. Let us look at a common statement we hear all the time. "I Love you." God has said He is Love so let us make, "I Love," the first variable. The second variable is who the Love is directed toward. That would be, "you." To make it easier to see I have added parentheses as arithmetic has taught us.

God is always pouring more love into our hearts.

Love Like Jesus

FIRST	SECOND
(I Love)	(You)
(∞)	(You)

$$\infty \times \text{You}$$

Love is equal to infinity, "∞." Notice how there is no end and no beginning. It loops around without end. This is the consistency and constancy of Love. Infinity times any non-zero number becomes infinity. God brings us into limitless Love! He multiplies His love based on how much our variable, "you," can receive. What is the value of your variable? The more you spend time with Him, the more you increase your own variable.

Infinity times zero equals undefined. This is why some people do not receive. They have turned off their receiver and changed their variable to zero, but through continued exposure to Love, this can be increased. It is a process of transformation by hearing the Word of God. We must be willing to share the Word of God in

Love instills passion to care for the needy.

Love.

> **Romans 10:15 VOICE —** 15 How can some give voice to the truth if they are not sent by God? As Isaiah said, "Ah, how beautiful the feet of those who declare the good news of victory, of peace and liberation."

We love God too much to ignore what He tells us. When I understood how much He loved me: that changed everything. He loves everyone in the same measure as He does me. Who would not want to know of this amazing love that satisfies our every need? I love His people, my brothers, my sisters, and my future siblings too much to ignore their needs. We would be doing them a disservice to not share the truth with them. We want them to know Him. We must see people after His own heart. He wants all humankind to know Him.

Love is unconditional. He loves everyone the same. For Him to heal, restore, set free, or deliver an unbeliever is for Him to showcase Love. God is Love and Love covers a multitude of sins.

> **1 Peter 4:8 NLT —** 8 "Most important of all,

Gifts of Love flow when moved by compassion.

continue to show deep love for each other, for love covers a multitude of sins."

Holy Spirit works through Love and all the gifts flow out of Love.

> **Galatians 5:6 TLB** — 6 And we to whom Christ has given eternal life don't need to worry about whether we have been circumcised or not, or whether we are obeying the Jewish ceremonies or not; for all we need is faith working through love.

It is not about us attempting to love others through our own self-imposed actions but rather letting God's love for them to flow out of us. That is when lives change and hearts are renewed. We learn to love like Jesus by seeing people after the Father's heart. We are vessels for Love to be poured out on others. Servant love is the greatest love and it is what Jesus modeled for us.

> **Matthew 20:28 ERV** — 28 Do as I did: The Son of Man did not come for people to serve Him. He came to serve others and to give His life to save many people.

> **1 John 3:16 VOICE** — 16 We know what true love

looks like because of Jesus. He gave His life for us, and He calls us to give our lives for our brothers and sisters.

Jesus is the Way. Following the path He demonstrated is love. What did Jesus do? What did He say? How did He behave? What were the results? The most excellent Way is Jesus.

Practical application:

Jesus: healed all who were sick.
Us: offer to heal others in His name.

Jesus: comforted those who were distraught.
Us: offer to comfort those who are ailing.

Jesus: blessed with His words.
Us: bless those around us with His words.

Jesus: gave of Himself freely.
Us: give and serve as He did freely.

Jesus: gave to the poor.
Us: provide needs for those and teach them

 *Love is practical and logical.*

about God's provision.

Jesus: cared about the needs of the people, fed 9000 men and their families.
Us: provide food for the hungry and give them the Word to trust God for their needs.

Jesus: met people where they were and brought them up to His level.
Us: go to where the people are and bring them up to His level.

Jesus: taught the Bible with authority.
Us: teach principles of the Word to others with authority.

Jesus: made disciples to carry on His legacy.
Us: make disciples to carry on His legacy.

Jesus: prayed to the Father for direction and listened for His voice.
Us: pray for direction and listen to Holy Spirit's voice and peace.

Love sees a need and fills it without question.

Jesus: operated in gifts through love.
Us: operate in gifts of Holy Spirit through Love.

That same Love dwells in You! Love wants to heal! Love wants to take care of you and others! Will you let Him? Will you accept what He has done for you? Salvation was provided by Jesus and it was because of Love. Healing was provided by Jesus and it was because of Love. Freedom was provided by Jesus and it was because of Love. Do you get the picture? Love has provided all things for us so that through Him we can love others the selfsame way He loves us. Let us go forth and love like Jesus!

Love teaches us to care for all especially our enemies.

CHAPTER 5
Love Forgives

Proverbs 25:21-22 tells us that if your enemy hungers or thirsts you are to care for them. You can only do this through Love! Then, it says that by doing so, it will heaps burning coals on his head. How is that good for them? Read the scripture below and you will see what I mean.

> **Proverbs 25:21-22 KJV** — 21 If thine enemy be hungry, give him bread to eat; and if he be thirsty, give him water to drink: 22 For thou shalt heap coals of fire upon his head, and the LORD shall reward thee.

This scripture always puzzled me. Surely by taking care of our enemy we are not hurting them, but then I heard that this is an Arabian expression. Heaping burning coals of fire on someone stands for the acute mental pain that is caused by them being guilty of the wrongs they have done to you. Your love, in contrast to their evil, awakens their conscience. Then they repent and seek to be reconciled.

> **Romans 12:17-21 NKJV** — 17 Repay no one evil for evil. Have regard for good things in the sight of all men. 18 If it is possible, as much as depends on you, live peaceably with all men. 19

Love displays mercy to all.

> Beloved, do not avenge yourselves, but rather give place to wrath; for it is written, "Vengeance is Mine, I will repay," says the Lord. 20 Therefore "If your enemy is hungry, feed him; If he is thirsty, give him a drink; For in so doing you will heap coals of fire on his head." 21 Do not be overcome by evil, but overcome evil with good.

This makes so much more sense in this context. We love others especially those who rub us the wrong way or we just do not see eye-to-eye with. By loving them, you show them a more excellent way. Your light dispels their dark. You make them hunger and thirst for righteousness. Your love, draws them to Jesus: they will realize they need a Savior!

> **Luke 9:51-56 NKJV** — 51 Now it came to pass, when the time had come for Him to be received up, that He steadfastly set His face to go to Jerusalem, 52 and sent messengers before His face. And as they went, they entered a village of the Samaritans, to prepare for Him. 53 But they did not receive Him, because His face was set for the journey to Jerusalem. 54 And when His disciples James and John saw this, they said,

Love does not get offended.

Love Forgives 150

> "Lord, do You want us to command fire to come down from heaven and consume them, just as Elijah did?" 55 But He turned and rebuked them, and said, "You do not know what manner of spirit you are of. 56 "For the Son of Man did not come to destroy men's lives but to save them." And they went to another village.

Just because someone is rejecting your faith or persecuting you does not mean you are not having an impact on them. Pray for them, believe for opportunities to bless them, and love them even when it is hard. Because Jesus loved the world even while they were crucifying Him. Surely, we can love those who persecute and hurt us. To show them love may be the reason you met that person in the first place.

If you love your enemies are they really your enemies? Love should be a constant. Humans can be easily manipulated. We should not let other humans hurt us to the point where we do not love them. Our true enemies are not humans. This is why prayer is important because it weakens the power of Satan and his minions. Sometimes the only thing God wants you to do in a situation is

God is able to reach others in Love through you.

pray and that is not a bad thing! Prayer is an exceedingly good action and does wonders. Praying in the spirit and/or praying with the natural mind can change circumstances quickly.

> **Ephesians 6:12 ERV** — 12 Our fight is not against people on earth. We are fighting against the rulers and authorities and the powers of this world's darkness. We are fighting against the spiritual powers of evil in the heavenly places.
>
> **2 Corinthians 10:4-5 VOICE** — 4 The weapons of the war we're fighting are not of this world but are powered by God and effective at tearing down the strongholds erected against His truth. 5 We are demolishing arguments and ideas, every high-and-mighty philosophy that pits itself against the knowledge of the one true God. We are taking prisoners of every thought, every emotion, and subduing them into obedience to the Anointed One.

Remember, we do not fight people but the spirits that influence them. One of Satan's favorite schemes is to divide the body of Christ. He can twist our words against others. He will try to get others to speak negatively about us. He will send

Love separates the person from the sin.

Love Forgives

gossipers and disguised wolves to sow discord. He is looking for those whom he may devour. One of the ways he does this is by testing us to see if we will get offended.

> **1 Peter 5:8 NKJV —** 8 Be sober, be vigilant; because your adversary the devil walks about like a roaring lion, seeking whom he may devour.
>
> **James 1:13 VOICE —** 13 No one who is tempted should ever be confused and say that God is testing him. The One who created us is free from evil and can't be tempted, so He doesn't tempt anyone.
>
> **Psalm 52:2 NLT —** 2 All day long you [Satan] plot destruction. Your tongue cuts like a sharp razor; you're an expert at telling lies.

We can make our lives extremely difficult by accepting offense or getting offended at another. Offense is not for us. When I think about the word, "offend," it sounds like a balancing term. When we are, "off," that means we are not, "on." We have taken a step off the solid foundation that is Jesus Christ the Cornerstone. This means that

Actions do not define a person, only Love can.

our ground becomes shaky; our balance is out-of-whack. We can be affected by things that normally would not have touched us. We can be knocked around and potentially fall! To be, "offended," is to be completely out of equilibrium.

We were not made to carry offense. It is a weapon of Satan's. He knows how to wield it skillfully. Little annoyances can grow into immensely large walls, and it can be so subtle in how it happens over time. The seed principle works in the negative. If we plant a seed of offense, it will grow unless we get Jesus to uproot it through forgiveness.

> **Ephesians 4:26 TLB —** 26 If you are angry, don't sin by nursing your grudge. Don't let the sun go down with you still angry—get over it quickly;

Offense (unforgiveness) is a form of death. It is the beginning stages of the death of a relationship. Death was not made for us therefore offense was not made for us. If you take on offense you are taking on the identity of Satan. We were not made in his image! We were made in God's image and therefore we shall choose to

Death was defeated by Jesus so we could live in Love.

Love Forgives

behave like Him! When we take on Satan's image, we get his fruit. His fruit is sickness, disease, fearfulness, frustration, pain, grudges, destruction, anxiety, chaos, depression, hardness of heart, laziness, greediness, immorality, impulsiveness, rudeness, harshness, impatience, and pridefulness just to name a handful! Does anyone want to willfully choose to partake of such terrible tasting fruit? No!

When we take on God's identity we will get His fruit. His fruit is love, joyfulness, peacefulness, kindness, goodness, faithfulness, self-control, meekness, patience, purpose, blessings, mercy, forgiveness, freedom, communion with God, healing, restoration, and authority to name a few! That sounds much better! Let us choose God's identity of forgiveness.

Offense can also come from a lack of believing that God loves you. I can hear some of you already saying, "But you do not know what they did to me! You have no clue on how much they messed up my life. They... [insert what is holding you captive]." You are correct, I may not know but Jesus does and He cares. Look what Hebrews tells

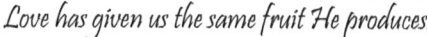

Love has given us the same fruit He produces.

us about our High Priest.

> **Hebrews 4:15 VOICE** — 15 For Jesus is not some high priest who has no sympathy for our weaknesses and flaws. He has already been tested in every way that we are tested; but He emerged victorious, without failing God.

Jesus lived a human life and experienced the same temptations we had. Yet, because He was able to keep His focus on the Father and Holy Spirit, He overcame them all without giving in even once. He saw people die. He saw people get sick. He saw people make bad choices. He lived life like we would. Temptation was all around Him. Satan tried to get Jesus to deny His divinity but Jesus knew who He was.

> **Matthew 4:4, 7, 10-11 NKJV** — 4 But He answered and said, "It is written, 'Man shall not live by bread alone, but by every word that proceeds from the mouth of God.' " ... 7 Jesus said to him, "It is written again, 'You shall not tempt the LORD your God.' " ... 10 Then Jesus said to him, "Away with you, Satan! For it is written, 'You shall worship the LORD your God, and Him only you shall serve.' " 11 Then the

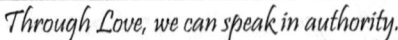

Through Love, we can speak in authority.

Love Forgives 156

devil left Him, and behold, angels came and ministered to Him.

He experienced a brutal and gruesome death at the hands of the creation He so loves. The creation that He lived with for around 30 years. The creation that He spent countless hours praying for, healing, delivering, setting free, and teaching. This very same creation He was destined to save is now excited to kill Him. Do you think there was room for Jesus to be offended? Do you think He could have a chance to think about how ungrateful these people are? I believe He could have but He did not. He was looking ahead to what was to come and not what was happening.

> **John 12:24 NLT —** 24 I tell you the truth, unless a kernel of wheat is planted in the soil and dies, it remains alone. But its death will produce many new kernels--a plentiful harvest of new lives.

As He was dying on the cross, He asked the Father to forgive the soldiers.

> **Luke 23:34 NLT —** 34 Jesus said, "Father, forgive

Love intercedes for others even when it hurts.

them, for they don't know what they are doing."
And the soldiers gambled for His clothes by
throwing dice.

You see, I believe Jesus had mercy on those soldiers. He knew they were not able to resist the commandment to crucify. He knew they might have enjoyed killing the, "Radical," who claimed He was the Son of God. Many soldiers could have volunteered to come that day just to gamble for His costly clothes to satisfy their greed. They may have thought they were doing a good deed by ridding the world of another pretender. They also could have been fearful as they were doing this, but to protect their lives they had to carry out the orders. Jesus recognized that it was not them at fault, it was the spirits behind them, and to quiet His own thoughts of possible offense, He asked the Father to forgive these men.

> **Psalm 65:3 NLT —** 3 Though we are overwhelmed by our sins, You forgive them all.
>
> **Psalm 86:5 VOICE —** 5 O Lord, You are good and ready to forgive; Your loyal love flows generously over all who cry out to You.

Love sees the good in every person.

Love Forgives

Jesus knows the true nature of the Father as Love. He knew forgiveness would be the correct response no matter what was trying to come out of the flesh. Jesus was demonstrating His position as the Mediator and Lover of humankind. Love truly and fully forgives wholly. While we were yet killing Jesus, He was already mediating on our behalf. That is the kind of loving God that we have chosen to partner with.

> **Romans 5:8 NKJV —** 8 But God demonstrates His own love toward us, in that while we were still sinners, Christ died for us.
>
> **Hebrews 8:6 ERV —** 6 But the work that has been given to Jesus is much greater than the work that was given to those priests. In the same way, the new agreement that Jesus brought from God to His people is much greater than the old one. And the new agreement is based on better promises.

Jesus forgave us so that we would have the ability to forgive others. We can only give what we have received. We must absolutely know beyond the shadow of a doubt that we are forgiven. If we have not allowed ourselves to reap

 Love amplifies louder than sin.

the benefit of forgiveness that Jesus died to give us, then we could never forgive another.

> **Colossians 3:13 NLT —** 13 Make allowance for each other's faults, and forgive anyone who offends you. Remember, the Lord forgave you, so you must forgive others.

> **1 John 1:9 NLT —** 9 But if we own up to our sins, God shows that He is faithful and just by forgiving us of our sins and purifying us from the pollution of all the bad things we have done.

We can only forgive through Love. There is no other way. No amount of science, talking about it, pharmaceuticals, drugs, will power, self-help books, religious, or spiritual acts can accomplish forgiveness. Forgiveness is a gift from God.

The unrenewed part of our souls wants to hold on to every perceived slight it has received. It wants revenge when it is treated unfairly. That part of us is the one we must deny through the power of Holy Spirit.

> **Galatians 5:16 VOICE —** 16 Here's my instruction: walk in the Spirit, and let the Spirit bring order to your life. If you do, you will never give in to

---

Love forgave all sin so we could do the same.

Love Forgives

your selfish and sinful cravings.

Forgiveness is a touchy subject. Just mentioning the term can invoke another's wrath. Yet the Bible is clear that we are to forgive each other for there are dire consequences if we do not.

> **Matthew 6:14-15 TLB** — 14-15 Your heavenly Father will forgive you if you forgive those who sin against you; but if you refuse to forgive them, He will not forgive you.

God knows that unforgiveness is detrimental for us. There have been studies done that show unforgiveness carried on for long periods of time stresses the body. It destroys the body from the inside. Unforgiveness is a root for disease. If you allow unforgiveness in your heart, you open up a vacancy for Satan to take residence in. He is not a good tenant! He will push the boundaries and steal more ground the longer you let him stay. He will destroy everything he puts his hand to. Do not allow him to put his hand on you! I have heard it said that unforgiveness is like drinking poison and expecting the other person to feel the

Love disciplines the heart to hear His voice.

effect of it. Unforgiveness is toxic!

Matthew 6:14-15 is part of the famous, "Sermon on the Mount." Jesus is teaching all the people what the God-life looks like. He is using many examples to demonstrate how people should act and what pleases God. The whole point of His diatribe is to get people to understand that it is impossible to do all these requirements. He wants people to see their inability and then seek the answer through God which He reveals as Christ Jesus. Look at the following verses.

> **Matthew 5:21-22 NLT —** 21 "You have heard that our ancestors were told, 'You must not murder. If you commit murder, you are subject to judgment.' 22 But I say, if you are even angry with someone, you are subject to judgment! If you call someone an idiot, you are in danger of being brought before the court. And if you curse someone, you are in danger of the fires of hell.

Jesus is revealing to the people it is not the action that matters as much as it is the attitude of the heart. I find it interesting that He is talking about anger here. Calling someone an unkind word could be considered defamation of character.

According to Legal Zoom [https://www.legalzoom.com/articles/differences-between-defamation-slander-and-libel] defamation is defined as: "a false statement presented as a fact that causes injury or damage to the character of the person it is about." How important a trustworthy reputation is! We have an entire branch of lawyers who specialize in defamation lawsuits. We must not be flippant with our words especially when we are acting emotional. However, we live in a fallen world and sometimes things happen that get us riled up. Jesus cautioned us not to, "be," angry. We are not to take on the identity of anger. Jesus even had a moment of anger.

> **Matthew 21:12-13 NLT —** 12 Jesus entered the Temple and began to drive out all the people buying and selling animals for sacrifice. He knocked over the tables of the money changers and the chairs of those selling doves. 13 He said to them, "The Scriptures declare, 'My Temple will be called a house of prayer,' but you have

God desires for us to remain in Love.

turned it into a den of thieves!"

Yet, He still remained sinless. He did not remain angry. He did not hold a grudge. He did not take offense. He took care of business, forgave them for their wrongdoing, and continued ministering in power. The Pharisees did take offense, became jealous of Jesus, and plotted to kill Him quickly.

> **Mark 11:18 TLB** — 18 When the chief priests and other Jewish leaders heard what He had done, they began planning how best to get rid of Him. Their problem was their fear of riots because the people were so enthusiastic about Jesus' teaching.

Let us not remain angry with people as Jesus showed us. For people are not the problem. Let us not take on Satan's form but instead take on Jesus' identity.

Back to Matthew 5:22. Cursing is even worse than speaking unkindly to another. If you curse another you bring the curse on yourself.

> **Genesis 12:3 NKJV** — 3 I will bless those who bless you, And I will curse him who curses you; And in you all the families of the earth shall be

Love only speaks blessing and goodness.

Love Forgives

blessed."

> **Ephesians 4:29 VOICE** — 29 Don't let even one rotten word seep out of your mouths. Instead, offer only fresh words that build others up when they need it most. That way your good words will communicate grace to those who hear them.

We were made in God's image (as I have mentioned a goodly amount of times!). God has blessed His creation. To try to be the judge brings all the judgment on you. We are telling God that He is not the judge when we attempt to fill His position. Judging another is disallowed. Only God is just and holy. He is the only one who can judge a person. We have no say in the matter although we can stand in the gap, pray for people, and petition God with His own words. He is faithful to stand by His words and will have the final say.

> **Hebrews 10:30 NKJV** — 30 For we know Him who said, "Vengeance is Mine, I will repay," says the Lord. And again, "The LORD will judge His people."

> **James 4:11 NKJV** — 11 Do not speak evil of one

Love exhorts, builds up, and encourages the heart.

another, brethren. He who speaks evil of a brother and judges his brother, speaks evil of the law and judges the law. But if you judge the law, you are not a doer of the law but a judge.

The specific curse in Matthew 5:22 verse relates to using condemnation to discourage another. We should never discourage another. Satan is in the discouragement business. Do you want to invite Satan to speak through you? I know I do not! Condemnation destroys people's lives. There is no condemnation in Jesus. We should be spreading Love and not condemnation. We have a choice to speak life or speak death. To speak death is to deal death. As you speak it, you splash it all over yourself. James has choice words about this process.

> **James 3:6, 8-12 NLT** — 6 And the tongue is a flame of fire. It is a whole world of wickedness, corrupting your entire body. It can set your whole life on fire, for it is set on fire by hell itself. ... 8 but no one can tame the tongue. It is restless and evil, full of deadly poison. 9 Sometimes it praises our Lord and Father, and sometimes it curses those who have been made in the image

Love speaks life over everyone.

Love Forgives

of God. 10 And so blessing and cursing come pouring out of the same mouth. Surely, my brothers and sisters, this is not right! 11 Does a spring of water bubble out with both fresh water and bitter water? 12 Does a fig tree produce olives, or a grapevine produce figs? No, and you can't draw fresh water from a salty spring.

We are not like that though. We speak life to those around us. Like Paul, we bless those who cause us harm.

Romans 12:14 NKJV — 14 Bless those who persecute you; bless and do not curse.

He reiterated it twice that we should bless and not curse. It is twice as important that we bless them and not curse them. To curse someone is to wish another dead. You may not think that is the purpose of it but when it comes down to it: death is the final result of cursing. We are not death dealers though! We are life givers and light bringers! We choose to be Love to others.

Back to Matthew 6:15. How can God not forgive us? We have to remember that Jesus was

God sings in Love and joy over His kids.

in the transitional period between the Old and New Covenants. His whole purpose for the Sermon on the Mount was to show people that they needed a Savior. People were not able to forgive because they did not have Jesus empowering their lives. He showed the people how impossible forgiveness is without God.

When it mentions in Matthew 6:15 that God will not forgive you because you refuse to forgive others it is relating to the fact that unforgiveness invites Satan to destroy the heart. There are people so wrapped up in unforgiveness that they cannot hear Jesus or receive from Him. A laborer will need to be sent to them to minister truth and grace to their heart. You also need to keep in mind that Jesus was not yet the Mediator for us. He had to speak plainly within the confines of the Mosaic Law. Jesus fit perfectly into the time period for His ministry operated as culture dictated.

After Jesus died, rose again, and ascended to Heaven, He was able to take His position as our go-between for us and the Father. He has forgiven all sin. He has wiped the slate clean. He has given us His righteousness so that we can

Forgiveness is showing Love.

Love Forgives

forgive others like He forgave us.

Romans 5:15 VOICE — 15 But the free gift of grace bears no resemblance to Adam's crime that brings a death sentence to all of humanity; in fact, it is quite the opposite. For if the one man's sin brings death to so many, how much more does the gift of God's radical grace extend to humanity since Jesus the Anointed offered His generous gift.

Hebrews 12:24 NLT — 24 You have come to Jesus, the one who mediates the new covenant between God and people, and to the sprinkled blood, which speaks of forgiveness instead of crying out for vengeance like the blood of Abel.

Acts 26:17-18 TLB — 17 And I will protect you from both your own people and the Gentiles. Yes, I AM going to send you to the Gentiles 18 to open their eyes to their true condition so that they may repent and live in the light of God instead of in Satan's darkness, so that they may receive forgiveness for their sins and God's inheritance along with all people everywhere whose sins are cleansed away, who are set apart by faith in Me.'

Nothing can separate us from Love, period.

No longer do we have to worry about, "Will God forgive me for [such and such]?" He already has through Jesus, His Son. His Grace has given us the power to defeat the lust of the unrenewed mind. Let us also show others that same forgiveness and grace that was poured out on us and deny unforgiveness and offense any power in our lives through the power of Love!

Love uproots every bitter root in the heart.

all your expectations.

CHAPTER 5

My Love Testimonies

I remember a tiny example of God's love toward me. I was walking to Subway during my lunch break. I did this about every other day. The weather was perfect and the sky was beautiful. I thanked God for the wonderful day. I looked into the sky and I saw a cloud. This was not a normal cloud. This cloud was unlike any I had ever seen before. As I watched this unique cloud: it began to change color! It cycled through a variety of colors.

    I was in awe of this wonder. I asked God what this was about and He said, "I did this for you because I knew you would enjoy it." Wow! That really touched my heart. My God loves me enough to rearrange the sky and cause some amazing wonder to pass by all just to show the scale of His love for me? I have never seen another cloud like that. It must have been imported from Heaven. This is the kind of God we love. This is the God that loves us more than we can even comprehend. This is the God whom I will forever thank for His unfailing and unconditional love toward me.

    Another example is when I was looking for a car. I was in the process of saving up to buy a car.

 God enjoys surprising you with Love gifts.

I was tiring of borrowing a family members' car or using Uber. I asked a few people what I should look for in a used car and how much would I need to save. I received varying answers. I looked up cars and started checking Craigslist to find a vehicle I could afford. I asked my Pastor for some tips. He worked in the car sales industry for many years. He gave me great advice on what to look for and how to check it out.

    I felt in my spirit that I would need a car soon. I started searching more and spent hours each day looking for a car. I even thought of leasing one. My Pastor, out of the blue, texted me saying a car was donated to the church and I could have it if I wanted it. He gave me the church member's name and I contacted them. The funny thing is, I dreamed I would be given a car and I remember telling God that I would like to be given one. I did not think too much of it, and it did not happen exactly as I expected but the result was undeniable. I was grateful to my Pastor and to God for supplying my need!

    I went with my brother-in-law to pick up the car and found that it was a great deal. The car fit

Love already knows what you need before you ask.

me perfectly. It drove nicely. It had a large amount of trunk space. It could seat four. It was a small car which would make parking easy. It had an automatic transmission. It was a match made by Heaven! They easily could have gotten over three thousand for it. The guy took immaculate care of it. Sure it had over 100K miles but it was well-maintained.

    I drove it home and was so overwhelmed with thanksgiving and praise to God. I got a little carried away on the drive home and got lost but that did not phase me. I even was able to gas it up. I took it to the BMV the next day and it was official. The car was mine. I took it to my auto mechanic and he could not believe I got it for free. It was in great condition. Only a few minor things we had to address but it all worked out.

    God has perfect timing when it comes to us. He knew I would need a car for the next phase of my life. He already had the need covered. He is a great Father! He loves us!

Matthew 7:9-11 VOICE — 9 Think of it this way: if your son asked you for bread, would you give him a stone? Of course not—you would give him

Praise and thanks comes out of an overflow of Love.

> a loaf of bread. 10 If your son asked for a fish, would you give him a snake? No, to be sure, you would give him a fish—the best fish you could find. 11 So if you, who are sinful, know how to give your children good gifts, how much more so does your Father in heaven, who is perfect, know how to give great gifts to His children!
>
> **James 1:17 TLB** — 17 But whatever is good and perfect comes to us from God, the Creator of all light, and He shines forever without change or shadow.

Another example is when I was getting my GED. I was nervous about taking public tests. When I was 16 years-old, I took the SAT and failed miserably which sucked all the life out of my confidence in test-taking. I did not know what to expect about the GED.

I was most worried about the writing portion of the test. I struggled to write under pressure. When I attended grade school, I was sometimes the last student to finish a writing assignment in class. It made me feel stupid and that something was wrong with me.

I was going to a GED training center for

Love makes hard things easier.

lessons. The purpose was for them to determine if I was ready to take the test. I met a nice middle-aged woman who showed me the formula for the writing section. I practiced it and understood what I needed to do. I was amazed how easy it came! Thank You Lord for faithful teachers!

    I was preparing to take the GED soon. I talked with my Pastor at the time about it. He said there are grants you can get for college. I did not know too much about that world, but he did because he worked for a college. He arranged a meeting for me and a financial advisor he knew. I took my GED, passed it with flying colors, and was now thinking about college.

    College was not in my future plans. I expected to get a job immediately doing whatever. I did not think my parents could afford to send me to college. I met with the financial advisor and was pleasantly surprised to find out that grants could cover all my college expenses if I qualified for them. He gave me brochures to look at for different career choices. He also told my parents and I to fill out the FAFSA from their website. That government form is required to determine what

Love shares wisdom and direction with you.

kind of financial assistance I can get from the government. He told me we can schedule another meeting after I fill out the FAFSA. We thanked him for his time and went home.

I filled out the FAFSA and found out I qualified for the full amount they give! I was elated! I told my parents and they were happy for me. We set up another meeting with the financial advisor. He looked at my FAFSA, smiled and asked what program did I want to enroll into. I chose the computer science one. He said he would set up a meeting with Gateway College for me to take my aptitude tests to see what level of classes I could start with. I thanked him for helping me out and we parted ways.

I took the aptitude tests and scored highly. I did not need remedial classes. I enrolled in Gateway Community and Technical College. The journey was stupendous! I met a gaggle of friends; even some I stay in contact with to this day. I took part in college events. I was President of the Honor Society there for two terms. I learned leadership skills and how to manage difficult personalities. I learned goal setting and project

Love propels us to success in every area of life.

planning. I even had the privilege of knowing one of my friends gave their heart to the Lord! I enjoyed every minute of my time there.

I was able to use the FAFSA Pell Grants to pay my way entirely through! I graduated with a 4.0 and received the J.D. Patton award which is given to two outstanding graduates ever year. I am thankful to God for leading me. I did not expect to go to college or get a degree. After the GED, I believed my future was murky at best, but God had better plans for me. He abundantly worked in my life throughout college and propelled me to unforeseen heights in academic mastery. Praise the Lord for His wisdom to excel with success!

> **Proverbs 3:5-6 VOICE** — 5 Place your trust in the Eternal; rely on Him completely; never depend upon your own ideas and inventions. 6 Give Him the credit for everything you accomplish, and He will smooth out and straighten the road that lies ahead.

God is faithful to lead us when we trust Him! He gives us wisdom to make all the right decisions to bring forth His purpose in our lives. He loves us that much!

 Love makes a way even when we cannot see one.

Here is one last example I would like to share. I was happily working as an Escape Room Game Master at Breakout. It was fun! My co-workers and I got along great! I was the trainer of a specific room that was new and popular. We were going through a transitional period while a new General Manager was taking over. I did not think too much of it.

I was at home and working a part-time job as a web developer. My brother-in-law came to my room's door and asked what I was doing. I told him I was working. He said I should start my own company. That statement jarred me. I shelved the thought and continued working after giving him what he needed.

This was not a coincidence. Two other people that I knew and respected said the same thing to me. I began seeking the Lord about it. He gave me an inkling that it was time to quit Breakout. I completely rejected the thought. I said, in my heart, "No way, I need this job because it is providing an income for me. How else will I help my family with bills?" He did not change His mind but I was not on board. I continued working at

Love sees the end from the beginning.

Breakout.

A short time later, I was invited to a worship night by my friend Stephanie. She was the one leading it. It was on a weekend and I was not working that day so I told her I would be there. The worship was intense. The presence of God was heavy and the prophetic was flowing. During a quiet moment, God told me clear as a bell, "I won't leave you stranded on an island. I will take care of you." My will melted and I conformed to His. I could deny it no longer; I had to quit Breakout Games.

I kept asking the Lord when should I put my two weeks notice in and got crickets. I did not get peace for awhile. I looked at the dry-erase calendar at work and one of the days stood out to me. I do not know what was special about that day but I had peace finally. I wrote a quirky message that stated that I was leaving by that day. I took a deep breath because this was actually happening. I was going to start my own company. I still had lingering doubts how it would all work but I chose to trust God's word to me.

Choose to trust Love and you will proceed in peace.

I brainstormed with family and came up with a company name. I even got a logo designed by one of my co-workers. Tessa is a super-talented professional artist. She did a great job with it. I began looking up what I would have to do to become a company. I did research and talked with people. I still had to figure out how to even get work! I was beginning to get overwhelmed with choices and decisions. I took a step back and waited for direction from the Lord.

I had a burning desire to buy a gift for every one of my co-workers. I thought that maybe this would be a way for them to see Jesus through giving. It was around Christmas time too. I took mental notes on what I heard them all speak. I decided I would get each an individual gift related to their likes. I began buying stuff on Amazon. It was so much fun finding gifts for each person! I wonder if that is how God feels when He blesses us with gifts?

When I gave gifts to each person, some became speechless, others were nearly in tears, others were ecstatic, and then there were those who simply said thanks with a smile. I was able to

Love excitedly shares Himself with others.

show them a picture of Jesus as I was exiting the company.

    The last day ensued: it was bittersweet. We had a Christmas party that included going to another Escape Room. We enjoyed it much. I said my goodbyes at the end of the night. Nearly tearing up but was able to suppress them. I had been working with some of these people for about a year and bonds were already built. I carpooled back to my vehicle. Said more goodbyes took a deep breath and remembered all the good times I had at the building. I tried not to cry but a few tears eked out. I knew it was time to start a new journey. I drove home thanking God for all that He brought me through.

    I still did not have any work coming in! I sought the Lord about what to do for work. He pointed out a website called Upwork. Upwork is a website dedicated for freelancers to find work and for clients to post jobs. It is a middle-man platform that connects freelancers with open jobs. I filled out a profile, made some pitches to clients, and then waited to see what would happen. I would check it several times a day

The plans Love has designed for you are all good.

looking for jobs I could help with. I made pitches to about five or so projects. The next day I received a message from one of the potential clients asking if I could jump on a phone call. I responded yes I could. We used the Upwork messaging system to communicate. He shared his screen to show me what was wrong. He asked if I could work on it today. I told him I could. He accepted my proposal and we still work to this day. That was the 1st of many clients that came through Upwork. Praise the Lord for being faithful to His words!

    I have never looked back since. My company is growing because of God and His love for me. He blesses me with new clients. He consistently comes through. He brings work to my doorstep! I am grateful for Him!

    We are not chasing after the blessing; the blessing is chasing after us! There are so many more examples I could share with you about God's love for me. I want to remind you... God loves you the same! I am confident that if you look back through your life you will see examples of Love.

 Love expects to see more victories.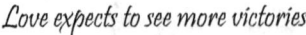

My Love Testimonies

> **Romans 1:20 NLT** — 20 For ever since the world was created, people have seen the earth and sky. Through everything God made, they can clearly see His invisible qualities--His eternal power and divine nature. So they have no excuse for not knowing God.
>
> **2 Corinthians 3:3 VOICE** — 3 You are the living letter of the Anointed One, the Liberating King, nurtured by us and inscribed, not with ink, but with the Spirit of the living God—a letter too passionate to be chiseled onto stone tablets, but emblazoned upon the human heart.

You might just surprise yourself with the sheer amount of God's loving telegrams you will be able to recall. Just like Paul, who experienced the love of God firsthand, you too will see how much God adores you when you examine your past. Love is evident in our testimonies!

Receiving Love in our hearts makes us want to testify.

CHAPTER

Love Gives Gifts

How great it is to know every need is met by our Heavenly Father. He so enjoys blessing others! I know He gets such a kick out of it. Love wants to prosper, bless, equip, encourage, and exhort all those around.

> **Ephesians 1:3 NLT —** 3 All praise to God, the Father of our Lord Jesus Christ, who has blessed us with every spiritual blessing in the heavenly realms because we are united with Christ.
>
> **2 Peter 1:2-4 NKJV —** 2 Grace and peace be multiplied to you in the knowledge of God and of Jesus our Lord, 3 as His divine power has given to us all things that pertain to life and godliness, through the knowledge of Him who called us by glory and virtue, 4 by which have been given to us exceedingly great and precious promises, that through these you may be partakers of the divine nature, having escaped the corruption that is in the world through lust.

Look at some of the benefits that Love has graciously provided for us!

New Heart [relationship]

We have a new heart in Jesus. When we put our trust in Him, He gave us His heart and

Love desires a fervent relationship with you.

resurrected our dead spirit. We can hear His voice. He enjoys speaking to us. What kind of Father would not talk to their children? Certainly not our Heavenly Father! He wants to guide us and help us at every point in our lives. The key is to drown out all other voices by focusing and meditating on the Word of God. There is an element of withdrawal from the world's influence. We have to make time for God in our lives. Any relationship that you build requires time. It is the same with our God. When you desire to know Him deeper, then you will make time for Him. I can tell you from personal experience... HE IS WORTH IT!

> **Ezekiel 36:26 NKJV** — 26 "I will give you a new heart and put a new spirit within you; I will take the heart of stone out of your flesh and give you a heart of flesh.

Will you make time for Me?

The Measure of Faith [manifesting the promises of God]

This is huge. We have the same amount of faith Jesus has. All have the same measure of faith. We put our trust in Jesus and He becomes

Love empowers faith to new heights.

our faith. He conquered all the power of Satan through His unwavering faith in the love of God. Jesus has no trouble believing the Father since He knows Him intrinsically and wholly. There is no doubt in Jesus' faith. When you put your trust in Jesus, you will get His results. He never fails. He never loses. He never backs down. Every demon trembles at His name. Every sickness loses its authority. Every weapon raised against Jesus is forcibly broken beyond repair. Believe on Jesus and salvation (complete life-wellness, body, soul, and spirit) shall be yours to have.

> **Romans 12:3 VOICE —** 3 Because of the grace allotted to me, I can respectfully tell you not to think of yourselves as being more important than you are; devote your minds to sound judgment since God has assigned to each of us a measure of faith.

Spiritual Fruit [identity]

The Fruit of the Spirit is the character attributes of Jesus. When we accepted Him, we also gained access to the same identity He has. He has no trouble loving in any circumstance. He has

God has given you all things needed to live life well.

received the love of the Father and bountifully shares with all. He dwells in peace as its Prince. He listens to the Father for perfect timing. He is the kindest and nicest being that has ever existed. He spreads goodness everywhere He goes. He is faithful to uphold His Word and deed. He is able to meet people where they are with a gentle spirit. He knows what He carries and teaches only what people can receive. Praise the Lord we are able to live just like Jesus! When people see you they can see Jesus because of the character you will exude.

> Galatians 5:22-23 VOICE — 22 The Holy Spirit produces a different kind of fruit: unconditional love, joy, peace, patience, kindheartedness, goodness, faithfulness, 23 gentleness, and self-control. You won't find any law opposed to fruit like this.

The Baptism of Holy Spirit [power to witness]

Jesus did not begin His ministry until He received the Baptism of Holy Spirit. He could not even start without the indwelling power of Holy

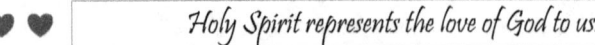
Holy Spirit represents the love of God to us.

Love Gives Gifts

Spirit. If Jesus needed Him, then we certainly do too! After I received the Baptism of Holy Spirit I was then filled with an insatiable desire to study God's Word. I had a deeper connection with Him. I was able to converse with Him easier. The writing and musical gifts He gave me came to the surface once I received the Baptism of Holy Spirit. Holy Spirit is a gift to us to empower us to live through Jesus. He is the fiery passion of Love that dwells on the inside of you.

If you have not yet chosen to welcome Him into your life, you are missing out on the absolute best God has for you. Once you welcome Him into your life (that's all it takes!), nothing will ever be the same again. Your love will be on a whole new level. Thank You God for the awesome Gift that is Holy Spirit!

> **Luke 11:13 NKJV** — 13 "If you then, being evil, know how to give good gifts to your children, how much more will Your Heavenly Father give the Holy Spirit to those who ask Him!"
>
> **Mark 16:17 NKJV** — 17 "And these signs will follow those who believe: In My name they will cast out demons; they will speak with new

Love communicates wisdom to and through us.

tongues;

Acts 1:8 VOICE — 8 Here's the knowledge you need: you will receive power when the Holy Spirit comes on you. And you will be My witnesses, first here in Jerusalem, then beyond to Judea and Samaria, and finally to the farthest places on earth.

Spiritual Gifts [power to serve others through Love]

The spiritual gifts are manifestations of God's great love for all. There are nine mentioned but I am under the impression there are more. God is always doing a new thing. We cannot box Him into our own self-imposed limits. He is able to do exceedingly, abundantly, above all that we ask or thing according to the power of Christ that flows through us! Each gift has a specific purpose in the moment. Any believer baptized in Holy Spirit can flow in any of the gifts. God brings them forth as needed. Be willing to submit your will to God because when He wants to bless someone through Holy Spirit... it is because He wants that person to experience His incredible love. Let us

Love desires us to serve and bless others.

Love Gives Gifts

always be on the look out for opportunities to be fountains of God's love to all!

> **1 Corinthians 12:7-10 VOICE —** 7 Each believer has received a gift that manifests the Spirit's power and presence. That gift is given for the good of the whole community. 8 The Spirit gives one person a word of wisdom, but to the next person the same Spirit gives a word of knowledge. 9 Another will receive the gift of faith by the same Spirit, and still another gifts of healing—all from the one Spirit. 10 One person is enabled by the Spirit to perform miracles, another to prophesy, while another is enabled to distinguish those prophetic spirits. The next one speaks in various kinds of unknown languages, while another is able to interpret those languages.

Power Over Sin [mercy, God's unmerited favor, live a holy life]

Thanks be to God that we no longer desire to sin! Our new heart has no disposition for sin. We have been set free by the grace of Jesus Christ. We no longer serve under sin but we serve under

Love conquers condemnation every time.

Jesus. We have a holy fear so to speak to please God in all that we do. Now, I want to make the distinction here, we are not trying to please God for His approval but because we appreciate and love Him. When you love another person you try to please them with your actions. It is the same way with God. We love Him and so we want to be pleasing to Him. God is so good to us. Sin's end game is death. God does not want us messing around with things that cause death! God has given us a better way to live through the power of the spirit. Grace has empowered us to live apart from sin, and to deny its urges and temptations. Hallelujah!

> **Romans 6:20-23 NLV —** 20 When sin had power over your life, you were not right with God. 21 What good did you get from the things you are ashamed of now? Those things bring death. 22 But now you are free from the power of sin. You have become a servant for God. Your life is set apart for God-like living. The end is life that lasts forever. 23 You get what is coming to you when you sin. It is death! But God's free gift is life that lasts forever. It is given to us by our

Love propels us to live a holy life apart from sin.

Love Gives Gifts

Lord Jesus Christ.

Divine Health [good life]

Jesus took away all sickness, disease, pain, encumbrances, and stumbling blocks when He humbly received lashings from the cat-o'-nine-tail whips the Romans used to torture Him. Jesus suffered immeasurable damage to His body. It is through that brokenness that He gives us wholeness. He exchanged all the suffering sin brought on us for His own divine life.

His life has no sickness, disease, or pain. His life has no broken heart, fear, anxiety, depression, or anger. His life delivers us from addictions, strongholds, wrong thinking, demonic entities, and curses. When we accepted Jesus, we accepted His life too! His life gives us all that we need to live divinely.

We never have to be sick again. We never have to be fearful again. We never have to be depressed again. We never have to be addicted to anything ever again. We can break down every stronghold, force out every demon, and break every curse through the power of Jesus' life. His

God wants us to enjoy life through His love.

life is healing and wholeness. If you have any needs in your body or soul then proclaim that by Jesus' stripes and His undeniable love for you that you are healed to wholeness.

> **Isaiah 53:3-5 NLV** — 3 He was hated and men would have nothing to do with Him, a man of sorrows and suffering, knowing sadness well. We hid, as it were, our faces from Him. He was hated, and we did not think well of Him. 4 For sure He took on Himself our troubles and carried our sorrows. Yet we thought of Him as being punished and hurt by God, and made to suffer. 5 But He was hurt for our wrong-doing. He was crushed for our sins. He was punished so we would have peace. He was beaten so we would be healed.
>
> **1 Peter 2:24 TLB** — 24 He personally carried the load of our sins in His own body when He died on the cross so that we can be finished with sin and live a good life from now on. For His wounds have healed ours!

The Mind of Christ [knowledge, creativity, revelation, wisdom, direction]

 Love only thinks good and pure thoughts.

Love Gives Gifts

Did you know you can think the same thoughts as Jesus? You have access to His holy mind through the spirit that dwells in you. You have access to the best search engine! In fact, it might as well be called the, "Answer Engine." No matter what you go through, you can draw on the wisdom of God for answers. He is able to show you what to do, when to do it, how do it, where to do it, and who to meet up with. He can give you as much detail as you need. Wisdom comes from the Lord who established it. Never can you say you do not have the answer because in Jesus you can get one!

> **1 Corinthians 2:16 NKJV** — 16 For "who has known the mind of the LORD that he may instruct Him?" But we have the mind of Christ.
>
> **1 Corinthians 1:30-31 NKJV** — 30 But of Him you are in Christ Jesus, who became for us wisdom from God--and righteousness and sanctification and redemption-- 31 that, as it is written, "He who glories, let him glory in the LORD."

The Blessings of Abraham [whole-life

Blessings from Love last for eternity.

prosperity]

    We are partakers of the covenant that God ratified through Abraham. Due to Jesus' sinless blood as a sacrifice for sin we are now united with the family of Abraham. We have become God's people which started with His covenant to Abraham. God knows how to bless His people! God promised many things to Abraham and He upheld every single promise. Look below to see some of the things that God promised him through Genesis 12, 13, 15, 17, and 22.

> You shall be a great nation. Your descendants will be more numerous than the dust of the land and stars in the sky. All the families of the earth shall be blessed by your Seed. I will make a covenant with you and multiply you. I will prosper and make you fruitful. Kings and nations shall be born from you. I make an everlasting covenant with you and your descendants. In blessing I will surely bless you and in multiplication I will surely multiply you.

    Israel was a great nation that ruled for 100's of

Love is confident in who He is and what He brings.

Love Gives Gifts

years before they fell away from the Lord. Spiritually, all the children of God are part of Abraham's family. Through Abraham's lineage, Jesus Christ was born. We have all received blessings through Jesus. He makes our way prosperous and fruitful. The works of our hands are blessed. Forever we shall dwell with God. The kingdom of Heaven is great and is growing in strength by the moment! Grace empowers us to live in the favor of God. All things will work together for good to those who call on the Lord and live knowing they are loved.

> I will bless you and make your name great.

Abraham is greatly emphasized in the New Testament as the forefather of all faith in God. Even when he lied to the kings who tried to take his wife as their own, God blessed him and protected him from their anger and fury. He blessed him more and made the others fear his power because God was with him.

> You shall be a blessing.

 Our Love walk draws others to Him.

The land prospered wherever he went. He was able to rescue his nephew Lot when he was captured with his own private army. He found wells in the desert and established them. He blessed Melchizedek with a 10th of all His wealth. He took no bribes or spoils from battles he won. He helped out others when they needed it. He was a good neighbor and friend.

> I will bless those who bless you and curse those who curse you.

Others made sure to not curse him or aspire to hurt him. He was blessed by his enemies. Other nations would ask to treaty with him because they saw God working on his behalf.

> I give you the land of Canaan. A place flowing with milk and honey. A place whose Maker and Builder is Me.

The promised land. Our promised land is Heaven but still we take dominion over the land of earth. For everywhere we go, we proclaim the goodness and love of God. Plants and animals flourish when God's Word is spoken and lived out.

Grace and Truth are revealed through Love.

Love Gives Gifts

We force evil to leave the atmosphere when we proclaim God's truth boldly.

> I will be Your Shield and Exceedingly Great Reward.

Looking to Jesus, this means that we shall be protected and provided for. We hold up the shield of faith which is Jesus and we are protected from every attack of Satan's. Through Jesus we have access to all the inheritance of Heaven along with the blessing and wisdom to access it, but the greatest reward, is truly relationship with God. We have access to the Father's throne room. We can come and go as we please because we are His children. We can speak and learn from Him as much as we want. There is no better reward than relationship with God! I GUARANTEE IT!

> You shall possess the gate of your enemies.

To possess the gate of the enemies means that we have the authority over them. We do not allow them in. We keep the gate shut. Through

Nothing can win against Love.

Jesus, we have been given all authority to overrule Satan's rule. Jesus told us that the gates of Hell would not stand against the revelation of who Jesus is. Jesus has won the victory over death and through Him we rule and reign in this life and in the one to come.

Blessings of the Mosaic Law [more prosperity!]

The blessings listed in the Old Testament law are now ours through Jesus' obedience. We could never earn the blessings due to our sinful natures. However, through Jesus' faith, we can have all the blessings and none of the curses! Look below to see what some of these blessings are from Deuteronomy 28.

> I will set you high above all the nations of the earth. All people will see the blessing of the Lord on your life. You shall be above and not beneath.

You will be an example to God's goodness. You will be the salt that makes them thirsty for God. You will be the light that dispels their dark. You are the city set on a hill and cannot be

Love makes us look good when we obey Him.

Love Gives Gifts

hidden from sight. You will never be buried by the world's ideals. God will raise you up to new heights.

> You shall be blessed in the city and blessed in the country. Any place you go the blessing follows you.

This covers just about everything. No matter where you go, favor shines upon you. You will get unparalleled deals and offers from others. God's divine appointments and alignments will become so evident in your life. The land about you will burst forth in new growth. People will flock to you because of God's hand on your life.

> Your kids shall be blessed.

Your lineage shall know the Lord. You will teach them to love God. You will discipline them to follow Him. You can have peace knowing that the same blessing that is on you will pass on to them. You will enjoy watching God bless them throughout their lives.

> Your work efforts will be blessed.

 Love has commanded a blessing on our storehouses.

You will be empowered to get things done efficiently. God will give you wisdom to do things better. He will give you ideas to innovate and to bring out new avenues of wealth. You will be a benefit to your company so much so that they will not be able to deny God's hand on your life. They will promote you and you will reach many. If you have a company then God will greatly increase your effectiveness. He will bring clients to your door. You will bring in more than enough wealth to cover all expenses and have more than enough to grow exponentially through His wisdom.

> Your home life will be blessed. You will always have more than enough food. Your storehouses will be blessed. Your living quarters and municipality will be blessed. God will multiply your children, your livestock. and your provision. His timing will be perfect for you to harvest all year long from His blessings. He will bless the things you put effort towards.

Wow! Your relationships with your family and friends will flourish. God will always provide more

Love makes every relationship better with age.

Love Gives Gifts

than enough food to satiate you and those in your care. He will bless your bank accounts, sources of income, businesses, ministries, vehicles, houses, and your possessions. All things your hands touch shall be blessed. When others in the world have trouble because of the economy or unforeseen financial issues, God will prosper you. He will teach you how to steward your finances well. You are not dependent on the world for your needs for you have made God your Provider. He will take care of His own no matter what the circumstances are. All desires the Lord has placed in your heart, will be blessed and shall bring forth success and victory.

> Your enemies will be defeated before you.

Those who rise up against you shall never win. Satan and all his evil minions are living in perpetual defeat. They have no hope of success. Trust in the Lord with all your heart and lean not to your own understanding. Victory is yours in Jesus! The Lion of Judah has never lost a battle and He never will.

Love defeats every obstacle in your way.

| You shall lend and not borrow. |

You will be a blessing to those who need help. You will lend money and time to those around you. You will not need any loans for the Lord has graciously given you more than enough for your needs.

| You will be the head and not the tail. |

You will be a leader. You have been blessed to lead others. As an example for Christ you shall rule and reign as a king because the King of Glory, Jesus, lives inside you. He will teach you how to steward the authority that is given to you. People will trust you. People will follow you. You will be a trailblazer that leads people far into the Lord's heart.

Love has given us so much! We are inundated on all sides by goodness and grace! We cannot be separated from Love! He is for us. He is working things out for our good because He cares about us.

Psalms 23:6 TLB — 6 Your goodness and unfailing kindness shall be with me all of my life, and

Love has made His home in us.

Love Gives Gifts

afterwards I will live with You forever in Your home.

Romans 8:31-39 TLB — 31 What can we ever say to such wonderful things as these? If God is on our side, who can ever be against us? 32 Since He did not spare even His Own Son for us but gave Him up for us all, won't He also surely give us everything else? 33 Who dares accuse us whom God has chosen for His own? Will God? No! He is the one who has forgiven us and given us right standing with Himself. 34 Who then will condemn us? Will Christ? No! For He is the one who died for us and came back to life again for us and is sitting at the place of highest honor next to God, pleading for us there in heaven. 35 Who then can ever keep Christ's love from us? When we have trouble or calamity, when we are hunted down or destroyed, is it because He doesn't love us anymore? And if we are hungry or penniless or in danger or threatened with death, has God deserted us? 36 No, for the Scriptures tell us that for His sake we must be ready to face death at every moment of the day—we are like sheep awaiting slaughter; 37 but despite all this, overwhelming victory is ours through Christ who loved us enough to die for

Jesus broke every barrier that kept Love from us.

us. 38 For I am convinced that nothing can ever separate us from His love. Death can't, and life can't. The angels won't, and all the powers of hell itself cannot keep God's love away. Our fears for today, our worries about tomorrow, 39 or where we are—high above the sky, or in the deepest ocean—nothing will ever be able to separate us from the love of God demonstrated by our Lord Jesus Christ when He died for us.

God is constantly imagining new ways to bless us. He is obsessed with us. He never stops thinking good about us. He is always ready to help us. Always willing to teach and guide us. He is patient with us knowing we are not perfect. He encourages us. He sends us love notes and love gifts. He protects us from what we cannot see or discern. Even on our worst day, He never thinks about deserting us or abandoning us. We have the best Father we could ever dream up. There is nothing that compares to our God and His love. God truly is the Ultimate Lover!

The Ultimate Lover is always thinking about you.

Lord of Love

My Prayer for You

B

As you have read, God is Love and He enjoys loving you. He wants you to know how much He cares for you. He wants you to taste and see how good He is. He desires to build a relationship with you so He can instruct, guide, and help you through life. He sent Jesus to save us from sin and to adopt us as His own.

We need Love in our lives. We cannot have peace or joy in this world without the encouragement that we receive from Love. He has chosen to love us unconditionally. Nothing we can do or say will affect His love for us.

My prayer for you is that of Paul's from Ephesians 3.

> **Ephesians 3:16-21 NLT** — 16 I pray that from His glorious, unlimited resources He will empower you with inner strength through his Spirit. 17 Then Christ will make His home in your hearts as you trust in Him. Your roots will grow down into God's love and keep you strong. 18 And may you have the power to understand, as all God's people should, how wide, how long, how high, and how deep His love is. 19 May you experience the love of Christ, though it is too

 Our love for others helps us to intercede for them.

My Prayer for You

great to understand fully. Then you will be made complete with all the fullness of life and power that comes from God. 20 Now all glory to God, who is able, through His mighty power at work within us, to accomplish infinitely more than we might ask or think. 21 Glory to Him in the church and in Christ Jesus through all generations forever and ever! Amen.

• It is my utmost desire that you continue in this non-stop journey of Love. That you will stoke a desire in yourself to know Love as fully and deeply as you can in this lifetime.

• That Love so overflows your very being that nothing can shake you off of the Cornerstone of Jesus Christ. That no offense and no unforgiveness can take root in a heart that is rooted in Love.

• No matter what comes your way, joy, peace, and wisdom shall always be near you.

• Love will empower you to share with others. You will boldly and passionately seek

Love fulfills every desire we could ever have in life.

My Prayer for You

the goodwill of all you come in contact with. Just as Jesus was moved by compassion that you also will be moved by compassion to destroy the works of Satan.

- Understanding Love will embolden you to seek out the promises of God and activate the blessings of God in your life through faith. Faith comes alive by knowing Love.

> Almighty God in Heaven, I thank you for these readers. Lord, I pray that they have a new perspective of Your incredible love. That the seeds of Love that have been planted in their hearts will germinate and grow into an everlasting harvest.
>
> I thank You, Holy Spirit, for guiding and directing them in unfailing truth and unconditional Love. God, that the love that You share with the Son and Holy Spirit will enliven, revitalize, and awaken every heart. Jesus, I thank You for

Love surrounds you with blessings.

opening the eyes of their hearts to see Your goodness, grace, and love in every circumstance.

I ask that every false belief that has entrenched itself in their hearts will be uprooted in the name of Jesus Christ! That no obstacle, stronghold, spirit, or other falsity can prevent them from receiving Your boundless Love! I proclaim that every hurt, wound, betrayal, breach of trust, and unforgiveness found in the heart is healed right now in the name of Jesus! No more shall they be bound by Satan's schemes to deactivate their Love walk! No more will they wonder if they are loved or forgiven by You. By the blood of Jesus Christ, sin shall have no more dominion over their lives.

They will walk with You, God, moment-by-moment knowing they are Yours and You are theirs. They will know that You so treasure them and want the best for

 Love heals every broken heart.

My Prayer for You

their lives. They will choose to trust You at all times with thankful praise. You will work mightily through their lives to bless others with Love.

Lord Jesus, if they ever stray from Love or what You have taught them that You will remind them all of Your loving words. That You will fight hard for them. That You will never give up on them for even a second. That they will not be able to escape Your all-consuming goodness, mercy, and love that You freely give.

I thank You, Father, for setting them apart for a time such as this. Holy Spirit, empower them to walk in all of Love's blessings to the utmost. I bless them in the name of the Father, the Son, and Holy Spirit. In Jesus' holy name, I commit this prayer. Amen.

Here is a personal prayer for you to speak from the heart.

 Love wants your heart above all else.

My Prayer for You

Heavenly Father, in the mighty name of Jesus Christ, I come to You. I thank You for all that You have taught me about Love. I thank You for seeking me out and lavishing Your love that I could not earn. I believe that You are Love and that You are for me. I trust in Your goodness to lead me along in perfect righteousness.

If there be any barriers that are preventing Love from penetrating my heart, Lord reveal them to me that I can receive healing and restoration. I desire to know You more and more each day. I choose to trust You in all circumstances.

Empower me to love others the same way You love me. I thank You for Your goodness in my life. I praise You for I am fearfully and wonderfully made. I have seen Your goodness all throughout my life and I am grateful. Thank You, Lord! In Jesus' holy name, I commit this prayer. Amen.

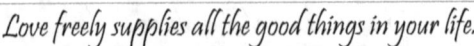

Love freely supplies all the good things in your life.

About the Author

Aaron Beach was born on March 4th, 1990 in Warsaw, Indiana. He was the 4th child to Joselyn and Douglas Beach and 1st boy. Five years later, his mother birthed a younger brother to complete the immediate Beach family.

Aaron grew up in church. Both of his parents were spirit-filled and active participants in church. His mother was a prolific song writer, pianist, prophetess, prayer warrior, and strong woman of God. She played the keys in every church she ever attended. His dad worked two sometimes three jobs to provide for the family. He was not home much during the early years of Aaron's childhood.

Aaron thought there was a God but did not commit his life to Him. He pretended to be a Christian in church. He would go to church with family, go to children's classes, go to Youth Group, and attend special events. It was not until Aaron was in the 5th grade that he gave His life to Jesus.

Aaron had been going to Youth Group since he was of age. He had friends there and enjoyed the club-like environment. The Youth Group was planning to go to an Acquire the Fire youth event

Love is knocking on the door of every heart.

held in Indianapolis. The entire Youth Group was hyped to go there. Aaron was assured that it would be a fun experience by all in the Youth Group. He asked his parents but they did not have the money.

He went to Youth Group expecting to not be able to go when the Youth Pastor, Nancy, came over. She said he was sponsored by someone in the church and would be able to go after all. It was a miracle of provision that brought Aaron there! He was excited to be able to attend. He packed the night before and was dropped off by his parents. The whole experience was fun.

On the last night, the News Boys were putting on a concert and they sang a beautiful song about the love of God. The atmosphere changed and became thick with the glory of the Lord. There was an altar call of which Aaron was too shy to go down. No one could tell he was not a Christian, he was not about to reveal it now! He was a good hypocrite! Aaron closed his eyes and had a life-changing encounter with God's love that transformed him. He could not resist God anymore. He chose to accept Him in his seat.

Life truly begins when Love is received.

About the Author

From that point on, Aaron's life was radically different. He cared about people. He did not care to play pranks or practical jokes on others. He no longer liked to lie. He desired to know God and enjoyed church for the preaching too.

God has been working mightily in Aaron's life. There are too many testimonies to recount. Aaron has had encounters with the Lord many times. Aaron went to Charis Bible College Indianapolis and got an Associate's degree in ministerial studies. He went to Crossroads School of Chaplaincy and became an ordained Chaplain. He has a website for encouraging the body of Christ at PraiseWithoutCeasing.online. His first book was published on March 4th, 2021 and is called 40 Days & Nights of Passionate Devotions (found on Amazon or free download on his website). He attends Discovery Church International (DCI.church) where he manages their website and Sunday media.

God has given Aaron a large vision to equip the Body of Christ with truth that empowers them to know God deeper, to fulfill the Great Commission, and to unite the true believers in

Love has equipped us with every spiritual blessing.

About the Author

Jesus to propagate change in the world. It is his prayer that you would seek God at all times, exercise your God-given gifts in love, and prosper in all the blessings He's provided, Grace and Peace to all of you. Thank you for supporting this ministry!

With all of Love's blessings,
Aaron Beach

 Love cannot be denied for He is Truth.

Get in Touch

We would love to hear what you have to say! If you have a testimony, a prayer request, or just want to say hi, you can visit our website at **PraiseWithoutCeasing.online** or email us at info@PraiseWithoutCeasing.online. If you would like to support this ministry you can give with PayPal or CashApp. Thank you for your support!

Scan to visit website

$narotosensei

paypal.me/aarbea

A joyful giver is the delight of Love's heart.

Search for Love

You may have noticed some pages had a faded out phrase in the background. This was by design! You can search for each phrase and write out the secret Love Letter God wants you to read! The whole point of this exercise is to show you that we can seek to know God more.

> **Jeremiah 29:13 NKJV** — 13 And you will seek Me and find Me, when you search for Me with all your heart.

Use the following page numbers and blank lines to spell out God's Love Letter for you!

_____	_____	_____
2	5	8
12	16	17
	20	23
	24	27
29	30	32

Love is calling out to you.

_____ 35 _____ 36

_____ 38 _____ 39 _____ 41

_____ 44 _____ 45

_____ 46 _____ 48

_____ 52 _____ 53

_____ 56 _____ 57

_____ 58

_____ 61 _____ 64 _____ 66

_____ 69 _____ 72

_____ 73 _____ 76 _____ 78

_____ 81 _____ 83

_____ 84 _____ 88

♥ ♥ *Seek Love first always.* ♥ ♥

_____
             89   92

_____
    93   95

_____
96   99   102

_____
       103   106

_____
    107

_____
   110   111

_____
112   114

_____
   116   119

_____
      122   124

_____
                 127

_____
     128

Love can soften the hardest of hearts with one word.

129		132	
133			134
	136	137	
	139		140
	143		145
	149	151	153
	156	157	159
		162	
163		166	
	169	170	

 Love defines the entire purpose of creation.

173	174		
175	178	179	
	180	183	184
	187		189
	192		193
	196		
198	199		
202	203	207	

THE ULTIMATE LOVER

Love looks over your life and is pleased with you.

www.ingramcontent.com/pod-product-compliance
Lightning Source LLC
Chambersburg PA
CBHW051425290426
44109CB00016B/1438